A CIVIL MATTER: A GUIDE TO CIVIL PROCEDURE AND LITIGATION

by

GEORGE W. KUNEY
Lindsay Young Distinguished Professor of Law
and
Director, James L. Clayton Center for
Entrepreneurial Law
The University of Tennessee College of Law

DONNA C. LOOPER
Adjunct Professor of Law
The University of Tennessee College of Law

WEST ACADEMIC PUBLISHING

Mat #41488636

The publisher is not engaged in rendering legal or other professional advice, and this publication is not a substitute for the advice of an attorney. If you require legal or other expert advice, you should seek the services of a competent attorney or other professional.

© 2014 LEG, Inc. d/b/a West Academic

444 Cedar Street, Suite 700
St. Paul, MN 55101
1-877-888-1330

West, West Academic Publishing, and West Academic are trademarks of West Publishing Corporation, used under license.

Printed in the United States of America

ISBN: 978–0–314–28905–6

ACKNOWLEDGMENTS

The authors thank Wendy G. Patrick, UT College of Law Class of 2013, for her significant contribution of time and detail-oriented effort to this project. It would not have been possible without her. Thank you also to Jordan Meetze, UT College of Law Class of 2015, and Amy Bergamo, UT College of Law Class of 2014, for proofing the manuscript and to Professor Paula Schaefer for her review and helpful comments along the way.

They also thank United States Magistrate Judge H. Bruce Guyton, who, through his former law clerk, Courtney Rodgers, recommended the case of *Neely v. Fox* for this project. Finally, the authors thank the attorneys involved in the case—Michael C. Inman, Robert J. English, and Clint J. Woodfin—for cooperating and sharing the trial transcript without which this project would have been impossible.

ABOUT THE AUTHORS

George W. Kuney is a Lindsay Young Distinguished Professor of Law and Director of the Clayton Center for Entrepreneurial Law at The University of Tennessee College of Law in Knoxville, Tennessee. He holds a J.D. from the University of California, Hastings College of the Law, an M.B.A. from The University of San Diego, and a B.A. in Economics from the University of California, Santa Cruz. Before joining the UT faculty in 2000, he was a partner in the Allen Matkins firm's San Diego office. Previously he practiced with the Howard Rice and Morrison & Foerster firms in his hometown of San Francisco, doing litigation and transactional work largely in the context of business restructuring and insolvency. He teaches a variety of business law courses and also writes extensively in that field. He is admitted to practice law in both California and Tennessee and consults in matters nationwide.

Donna C. Looper is an Adjunct Professor of Law at The University of Tennessee College of Law, Knoxville, Tennessee, where she teaches Legal Process. She received her J.D. from the University of California, Hastings College of the Law and her B.A. from Barnard College, Columbia University. She clerked for the Chief Judge of the United States District Court for the Eastern District of Louisiana and then for the United States Court of Appeals for the Ninth Circuit. Before teaching at the University of Tennessee College of Law, Ms. Looper was a Senior Attorney for the California Court of Appeal, Fourth District, Division One and, prior to that, was in private practice in San Diego and San Francisco. She is admitted to practice law in both California and Tennessee and consults in matters nationwide.

ALSO BY THE AUTHORS

Kuney:

Business Reorganizations (3rd ed. Lexis 2013, with Michael Gerber and Edward Janger).

Judgment Enforcement in Tennessee (Amazon/ Center for Entrepreneurial Law 2013, with Wendy G. Patrick).

The Entrepreneurial Law Clinic Handbook (West 2012, with Brian K. Krumm).

Bamboozled? Anatomy of a Bankruptcy: Baystate v. Bowers and Its Aftermath, (West 2012).

Contracts: Transactions and Litigation (3rd ed., Thompson/West 2011, with Robert M. Lloyd).

The Elements of Contract Drafting With Questions and Clauses for Consideration (3rd ed., Thompson/West 2011).

Sales, Negotiable Instruments, and Payment Systems: UCC Articles 2, 3, 4, and 5 (Center for Entrepreneurial Law 2010, with Robert M. Lloyd).

Secured Transactions: UCC Article 9 and Bankruptcy (Center for Entrepreneurial Law 2009, with Robert M. Lloyd).

Mastering Bankruptcy Law (Carolina Academic Press 2008).

Legal Drafting: Process, Techniques, and Exercises (2d ed., Thompson/West 2007, with Thomas R. Haggard).

Legal Drafting in a Nutshell (3rd ed., West 2007, with Thomas R. Haggard).

Chapter 11–101: The Essentials of Chapter 11 Practice (ABI 2007, with Jonathan P. Friedland, Michael L. Bernstein, and Professor John D. Ayer).

Kuney & Looper:

California Law of Contracts (CEB 2007–2014, updated annually).

Mastering Appellate Advocacy and Procedure (Carolina Academic Press 2011).

Mastering Legal Analysis and Drafting (Carolina Academic Press 2009).

Mastering Intellectual Property Law (Carolina Academic Press 2008).

OUTLINE

TABLE OF CASES

References are to Pages

A CIVIL MATTER: A GUIDE TO CIVIL PROCEDURE AND LITIGATION

CHAPTER 1

NEELY V. FOX OF OAK RIDGE: EVENTS UNDERLYING THE CIVIL MATTER

I. THE ACCIDENT

On the afternoon of July 12, 2004, Thomas Neely was driving his Kia Sephia on State Route 61 in Anderson County, Tennessee. Complaint [407], ¶ 3; Answer [467], ¶ 3. Benjamin Curd was behind him, driving a 1998 Chevrolet Van. Complaint [407], ¶ 4; Answer [467], ¶ 4. The van was owned by Curd's employer, Fox of Oak Ridge. Curd had taken the van for repairs and was returning it to Fox. Trial Transcript ("TT") Vol. 2, pp. 43–44 [525]. It was raining, and, as Neely approached Park Avenue, a street leading into a shopping mall, he came to an almost full stop. According to Neely, he stopped to allow the car ahead of him to turn into the mall. Curd testified that he tried to stop, but that his van slid into the back of Neely's car, knocking it two to three feet ahead. The impact broke the car's front seat—leaving Neely "looking up at the ceiling of his car." TT, Vol. 2, pp. 5–6, 36, 43–54 [511]. Curd got out of the van, saw Neely in the broken seat, and called an ambulance. TT, Vol. 2, pp. 46, 52 [510]. Neely was taken to the Oak Ridge Methodist Medical Center Emergency Room and released the same day because he said he would see his doctor the following day. TT, Vol. 1, p. 106 [592]. The extent and cause of Neely's injuries and their impact on his earning capacity were central issues in the case. At the time of trial, Neely had not worked for two years—not since the day of the accident. TT, Vol. 2, pp. 39–40 [553].

II. SETTLEMENT NEGOTIATIONS

The precipitating events in the case were pretty simple and straightforward, as was the theory of liability—negligence. In short, the law imposes a duty upon everyone to act reasonably towards others in order to avoid damaging them. If one drives negligently or recklessly, one can be held liable for the damages that one causes to others. Of course the law is more complicated than that, as you will learn in torts class, but that is the gist of the matter.

Many times, cases like this are settled before trial or even before filing suit. In this case, however, it appears that prelitigation settlement discussions went nowhere or were nonexistent. *See* TT, Vol. 2, pp. 80–82 [554]. As you read this book and review the documents and transcripts in the docket, ask yourself why this case went all the way to trial and what issues might have kept the parties from settling?

The next chapters of this book follow the case from the filing of the complaint to post-trial, noting the substantive and procedural issues along the way. The purpose of this tour through a routine civil matter is to give the reader an overview of the process. Although a more detailed study of each of the stages of the case and the issues involved is needed to fully understand the civil justice system, the narrative description contained in this "guided tour" combined with the linked source documents and authorities provides the reader an overview of the civil litigation process sufficient to orient the reader for more productive future study.

CHAPTER 2

INITIATING A CIVIL ACTION

I.   OVERVIEW

A civil action is initiated by filing a document called a "complaint" in the proper court, which is known as the "forum." The complaint is the initial "pleading" that is filed to frame the issues for the court to consider. Therefore, it should contain every allegation necessary to entitle the plaintiff to the relief that she requests. As a result, visualizing what one must prove at trial is one way to test the sufficiency of the complaint. Thinking about the end game before making the first move is the best practice.

Attorneys must investigate the facts, review applicable law, and consider several specific issues before filing a complaint. First, the complaint must be filed within the time limit set out in the applicable "statute of limitations," otherwise all recovery will be barred. The complaint also must be filed in the correct court—that is, the court:

(a) with the power to decide the issues presented in the action—known as "subject matter jurisdiction;"

(b) with the power over the parties involved in the action—known as "personal jurisdiction;" and

(c) in the correct geographical area or "venue."

II. STATUTES OF LIMITATIONS

Statutes of limitations are laws that set time limits within which civil actions must be brought, if they are to be brought at all. These time limits (1) help ensure that suits are brought when memories are fresh and evidence is still available and (2) prevent the prospect of a lawsuit from "hanging over one's head" indefinitely – allowing the parties to get on with their lives. Generally statutes of limitations begin to "run" once the loss or injury has or should have been discovered. The time limits in statutes of limitations depend on the type of injury or claim involved. For example, a person may have less time to file a personal injury action than a breach of contract action. Thus, it is important for attorneys to be familiar with the statutes of limitations that are applicable and to ensure that they meet those deadlines, as actions filed after those time limits are barred.   In *Neely v. Fox*, applicable statutes of limitations could include TENN. CODE. ANN. § 28–3–104 [495] and § 28–3–105 [496].

QUESTIONS

1. Read Tenn. Code. Ann. § 28–3–104 [495] and § 28–3–105 [496]. What type of injury does each statue involve?

2. How long would Mr. Neely have to file suit under each statute?

III. SUBJECT MATTER JURISDICTION

Subject matter jurisdiction refers to the power of a particular court to hear the type of case involved.

For example, many states have separate civil and criminal court systems. In those states, a civil court would not have subject matter jurisdiction over criminal cases and vice versa. In the United States, there are systems of state courts in each individual state, as well as a system of federal courts throughout the country. Federal courts exist in every state, but Congress has given those courts the power to hear only certain types of cases—that power is called "federal subject matter jurisdiction." The three main categories of federal subject matter jurisdiction in civil actions are (1) federal question jurisdiction, (2) diversity jurisdiction, and (3) admiralty jurisdiction. Federal question jurisdiction is the power of a federal court to hear cases arising under federal law, which is defined as "the Constitution, laws, or treaties of the United States." 28 U.S.C. § 1331 [16]. Diversity jurisdiction refers to the power of a federal court to hear controversies between citizens of two different states, when the amount in controversy exceeds, currently, $75,000. 28 U.S.C. § 1332 [17]. Admiralty jurisdiction is concerned with maritime activities and actions. 28 U.S.C. § 1333 [23]. For further discussion regarding federal subject matter jurisdiction, *see* Chapter 3, section II(b), p. 24.

Subject matter jurisdiction may *not* be conferred by consent of the parties. A court either has the power to hear a particular type of controversy or it does not. That is a matter for the appropriate legislature, not the parties, to determine.

Question: Is there federal subject matter jurisdiction in *Neely v. Fox*?   If yes, under what theory?

IV. PERSONAL JURISDICTION

A court must also have power over the parties in the lawsuit such that it can enter a valid judgment against them.   This is known as "personal jurisdiction." Generally, for a state or federal court to have personal jurisdiction over a party, the party must reside in or have sufficient "minimum contacts" with the state in which the legal action is filed.   *International Shoe Co. v. Washington*, 326 U.S. 310, 316 (1945) [79]. Those minimum contacts between the defendant and the forum state must be of such a nature and quantity that an assertion of personal jurisdiction does not offend "traditional notions of fair play and substantial justice." *Id.* [79] Generally, courts look to whether there was "'some act by which the defendant purposefully avail[ed] itself of the privilege of conducting activities within the forum State, thus invoking the benefits and protections of its laws.'"   *Goodyear Dunlop Tires Operations, S.A. v. Brown*, 131 S.Ct. 2846, 2854 (2011) [6] (quoting *Hanson v. Denckla*, 357 U.S. 235, 253 (1958) [85]). Note that parties may consent to personal jurisdiction in a particular forum or court, which they cannot do with subject matter jurisdiction.   For further discussion regarding personal jurisdiction, *see* Chapter 3, section II(c), p. 27.

Question: In which state would courts have personal jurisdiction over the individuals and entities in *Neely v. Fox*? Why?

V. VENUE

While jurisdiction involves the power of a court to hear a controversy and enter judgment against a party or parties, venue refers to the geographic location of the court in which the civil action is filed. Generally, for venue to be proper, the action must be filed in the county (in most state systems) or district and division (in the federal system) in which

(1) the defendants reside;

(2) a substantial part of the events giving rise to the action occurred; or

(3) a substantial part of the property at issue in the action is located.

See, e.g., 28 U.S.C. § 1391 [25].

For a map showing all the circuits and districts in the federal court system, click here [643]. Notice that many states are divided into more than one district. For instance, in Tennessee, where *Neely v. Fox* was filed, there are three different districts.

VI. THE COMPLAINT

Civil legal actions are commenced by filing a "complaint" in the proper court. *See* FED. R. CIV. P. 3 [248]. Complaints are filed in the court's clerk's office, where the matter is assigned a case number and a case file is started. A court's list or index of the documents contained in the case file is known as a "docket sheet" or the "docket." To see the docket sheet in *Neely v. Fox*, click here [156].

One way of thinking about a civil action is to think of it as a file or series of files kept by the court. The party filing the complaint is invoking the court's jurisdiction to resolve the dispute. The court opens a file on the matter, and all the documents that the parties submit go into that file. A court in the American system is a rather passive entity under normal circumstances. It is up to the parties to file motions or take other actions that ask the court to make determinations and grant relief. The parties must tell the court the relief they want, state the applicable rule that says the court can grant that relief, show that the requirements of that rule are met and, thus, they qualify for that relief. The other side can then try to show that either a different rule applies or the requirements of the rule have not been met. The court then decides who is right and either grants or denies the requested relief. If the case goes to trial, each side attempts to convince the jury that the facts and the law, which is explained in a series of jury instructions, entitle them to prevail. This is the basic structure of the American adversary system of civil justice. When the case is over, the court closes the file. If the court's final ruling is appealed to a higher court, the file is, essentially, transferred to the higher court for review and a ruling.

Because a civil action is commenced by the filing of a complaint, the date the complaint is filed usually determines whether the applicable statutes of limitations have been met. In addition to initiating the action, a proper complaint gives the defendants and the court sufficient notice of the jurisdictional basis for the action, the claims, their underlying facts, and the relief sought. Both the federal and state systems have specific rules governing the content and form of complaints. For example, complaints filed in federal courts must contain

> (1) "a short and plain statement of the grounds for the court's jurisdiction,"
>
> (2) "a short and plain statement of the claim[s] showing that the pleader is entitled to relief," and
>
> (3) "a demand for the relief sought[.]"

FED. R. CIV. P. 8(a) [363].

The plaintiff may set out as many claims as she has—even if the claims are inconsistent. FED. R. CIV. P. 8(a) [363]. Thus one claim may be based on fraud or other deliberate conduct, while another is based on negligence. At some point in the case, the plaintiff will have to choose to pursue only consistent claims that are supported by the proof, but not at the outset of the case.

The first page of a complaint must contain a caption [144] naming the court and all defendants to the action, and all claims must be set out in numbered paragraphs, "each limited as far as practicable to a single set of circumstances." FED. R.

CIV. P. 10(a) & (b) [173]. A complaint or any other pleading or motion filed in federal court must be signed by at least one attorney of record or the parties themselves, if they are unrepresented by an attorney. FED. R. CIV. P. 11(a) [176]. Under Rule 11, by filing or otherwise "presenting" a pleading or motion to the court, the attorney or unrepresented party certifies that, to the best of his or her "knowledge, information, and belief, formed after an inquiry reasonable under the circumstances," the pleading or motion:

(1) is not filed for harassment purposes,

(2) does not contain frivolous claims or arguments, and

(3) is not lacking in factual basis or reasonable investigation of the facts.

An attorney or unrepresented party may be sanctioned (usually fined a sum of money) for failure to comply with Rule 11 [175].

The care with which a complaint should be drafted should not be minimized. The complaint (and the other side's answer to the complaint) will frame the issues in the case and establish whether or not the requested relief or judgment will be issued. These pleadings will define the issues that will be the subject of any trial or other dispositive hearing in the case. If a necessary allegation is omitted from the complaint, the complaint can be dismissed or the issue may not be allowed to be the subject of trial. The rules of modern pleading are more liberal and loose than their more formal ancestors, which were notoriously technical. However, great care should be taken at the pleading stages of the case to ensure that the parties are setting up their right to have the dispute determined as they desire. Some attorneys recommend writing out the jury instructions that one wants to use at trial and then drafting the allegations of the complaint so that they support them. In other words, visualize where you want to go and draft the complaint as a method, a tool, for getting you there.

On June 17, 2005, Mr. Neely's counsel filed his complaint [407] against Fox of Oak Ridge, Inc. and Benjamin H. Curd in the United States District Court for the Eastern District of Tennessee, Northern Division.

QUESTIONS

Statute of Limitations

1. What type of injuries does Mr. Neely allege?

2. Does Mr. Neely allege any injury to property?

3. Based on the type of injury alleged, which Tennessee statute of limitations applies, TENN. CODE ANN. § 28–3–104 [495] or § 28–3–105 [496]?

4. Was Mr. Neely's complaint filed within the applicable statute of limitations? Why?

Jurisdiction and Venue

1. Which paragraph(s) of the complaint contain(s) allegations regarding federal subject matter jurisdiction?

2. Federal subject matter jurisdiction is alleged based on what theory?

3. Based on your knowledge so far of the facts and the law, did the court have subject matter jurisdiction in *Neely v. Fox*? Why?

4. Which paragraph(s) of the complaint contain(s) allegations regarding the personal jurisdiction over Fox of Oak Ridge, Inc. and Benjamin Curd?

5. Assuming the allegations are correct, did the court have personal jurisdiction over Fox of Oak Ridge, Inc. and Benjamin Curd? Why?

6. Based on the location of the accident and the locations or residences of the defendants, was venue proper? Why?

Claims and Demand for Relief

1. Which paragraphs of the complaint involve Mr. Neely's claims for relief and their factual bases?

2. What paragraph contains allegations that describe Mr. Neely's actions?

3. What paragraphs contain allegations describing Mr. Curd's actions?

4. What paragraphs contain legal theories for relief?

5. What paragraph alleges that Mr. Curd was "negligent per se" based on his alleged violation of two Tennessee statutes?

6. Does the complaint allege that Mr. Curd caused Mr. Neely's injuries or damages? Where? Which paragraph(s)?

7. Which paragraph alleges that Fox of Oak Ridge, Inc. should also be liable for Mr. Curd's alleged negligence?

8.   Which paragraph alleges Mr. Curd was acting in "the scope of his employment."

9.   Where in the complaint is the demand for relief? What relief is demanded?

Federal Rules Regarding Content and Form of the Complaint

1.   Does the complaint in *Neely v. Fox* meet the content requirements set out in FED. R. CIV. P. 8 [360]? Why?

2.   Does the complaint in *Neely v. Fox* meet the form requirements set out in FED. R. CIV. P. 10 [172]? Why?

3.   Based on what you know so far of the facts and law, does the complaint comply with FED. R. CIV. P. 11 [175]? Why?

VII. SUMMONS AND SERVICE OF PROCESS

When the complaint is filed, a court clerk will usually issue a summons [430] for each named party. The document itself is most often filled out by the plaintiff's attorney—the clerk "issues" the summons by signing it. A summons is directed to a specific defendant and contains the name of the court in which the complaint was filed, the names of the parties, and the address of the plaintiff's attorney or unrepresented plaintiff. The summons informs defendants that they must respond to the complaint within a specific time and that the failure to respond will result in a default judgment being entered against them for the relief demanded in the complaint. *See* FED. R. CIV. P. 4(a) [311]. The summons along with a copy of the complaint is then served on the defendant. In the federal and many state systems, any person who is over the age of 18 and not a party to the action may serve the summons and complaint. *See* FED. R. CIV. P. 4(c) [313]. Under Rule 4(m) [322] the plaintiff generally has 120 days after the complaint is filed to effect service.

Ideally, the summons and complaint are served directly, that is, by handing them to the individual defendant personally, to an officer of a corporate defendant, or to the registered agent for service of process. In certain circumstances "substitute service" is allowed by delivering the summons and complaint to a suitable person at the defendant's "usual place of abode." *See* FED. R. CIV. P. 4(e) [315]. In limited circumstances, service also may be made by publishing notice of the action in a newspaper of record for a prescribed period of time. Note that Federal Rule of Civil Procedure 4 [289] does not contain a specific provision regarding service by publication but provides that service may be made under the procedures allowed by the law of the state in which the federal district court is located. FED. R. CIV. P. 4(e) [315]. Many states provide for service by publication under specified circumstances. *See, e.g.* CAL. CODE. CIV. P. § 415.50 [141]; FLA. STAT. § 49.011 [166]; 735 ILL. COMP. STAT. 5/2–206 [119]; TEX. FAM. CODE ANN. § 102.010 [504].

Once a defendant has been served with the summons and complaint, proof of service must be made to the court. This is usually accomplished by filing a "return of service" in which the process server specifies when and how the defendant was served, and declares under penalty of perjury that the information is true and correct.   Review the summons (Fox of Oak Ridge [430] and Curd [440]) in *Neely v. Fox* and answer the following questions.

QUESTIONS

1. When were the summons and complaint served on Benjamin Curd?

2. How were the summons and complaint served on Mr. Curd?

3. When do you think the summons and complaint were served on Fox of Oak Ridge?

4. How were the summons and complaint served on Fox of Oak Ridge and on whom?

5. According to the complaint, who is Lester Fox?

CHAPTER 3

RESPONDING TO A CIVIL ACTION

I. OVERVIEW

Once the summons and complaint have been served, defendants are given a limited time to respond. If they fail to do so, plaintiffs may seek to have a "default judgment" entered against them for up to the amount demanded in the complaint. *See* FED. R. CIV. P. 55(a) [332] & (b) [333]. The amount of time allowed to respond to a complaint is governed by procedural and court rules. In the federal system, a defendant now has 21 days after being served with the summons and complaint to respond to the lawsuit. FED. R. CIV. P. 12(a) [179]. When the complaint was filed in *Neely v. Fox* the defendant had 20 days. In computing time to respond under the federal rules,

(1) exclude the first day—the day on which the summons and complaint are served;

(2) then count every day, including intervening Saturdays, Sundays, and legal holidays; and

(3) include the last day of the period, unless it is a Saturday, Sunday, or legal holiday, in which case the period continues to run until the next day that is not a Saturday, Sunday, or legal holiday. FED. R. CIV. P. 6(a)(1) [353].

Under the local rules in many federal districts, the time to respond to the summons and complaint may be extended by consent of the parties. For example, in the Eastern District of Tennessee, where *Neely v. Fox* was filed, "If all counsel agree, parties shall be entitled to a 21 day initial extension of time in which to respond to the complaint . . . ." E.D. TENN. L.R. 12.1 [158].

Generally, defendants may respond to a civil complaint in two ways: (1) by filing a motion to dismiss the complaint; or (2) by filing an answer to the complaint, which may also contain counterclaims against the plaintiff and cross-claims against other defendants.

II. RESPONDING BY FILING A MOTION TO DISMISS: FEDERAL RULE OF CIVIL PROCEDURE 12(b)

A.   OVERVIEW

The federal system and most state systems allow defendants to file a motion to dismiss on specified grounds prior to or in lieu of filing an answer to the complaint. Under Federal Rule of Civil Procedure 12(b) [180], a defendant may move to dismiss the complaint on the following grounds:

(1) lack of subject-matter jurisdiction;

(2) lack of personal jurisdiction;

(3) improper venue;

(4) insufficient process;

(5) insufficient service of process;

(6) failure to state a claim upon which relief can be granted; and

(7) failure to join an indispensable party under Federal Rule of Civil Procedure 19 [211].

Motions under subdivisions (1)–(5) and (7) of Rule 12(b) [180] are based on procedural grounds, while motions under Rule 12(b)(6) [187] are substantive and involve a challenge to the sufficiency of the underlying claims. Essentially, a Rule 12(b)(6) [187] motion argues that even if the plaintiff were to prove that the allegations of the complaint were true, the law would not allow or provide any relief to the plaintiff. Note that a motion to dismiss under 12(b) [180] may be based on more than one ground. As with any pleading or motion filed in federal court, a motion to dismiss under Rule 12(b) [180] is subject to Rule 11 [175]. Thus, in filing the motion, the attorney or unrepresented party certifies that, to the best or his or her "knowledge, information, and belief, formed after an inquiry reasonable under the circumstances:" the motion:

(1) is not filed for "improper purpose, such as to harass, cause unnecessary delay, or needlessly increase the cost of litigation,"

(2) does not contain frivolous claims or arguments, and

(3) is not lacking in factual basis or reasonable investigation of the facts.

FED. R. CIV. P. 11(b) [177].

When drafting a motion, it is often best practice to first draft the form of order that one wants the court to issue if it grants the motion. This focuses the drafter on the precise relief sought. Then one can identify, in the motion, the applicable rules of law and the pertinent facts that satisfy the legal rules and standards in explaining to the court why the relief sought in the proposed order should be granted.

B.   RULE 12(b)(1)—LACK OF SUBJECT MATTER JURISDICTION

As discussed in Chapter 2, subject matter jurisdiction refers to the power of a court to hear the type of case or controversy before it. Motions under Rule 12(b)(1) [181] are based on lack of federal subject matter jurisdiction. Only certain civil actions may be heard in the federal court system. The maximum bounds of federal subject matter jurisdiction are set out in Article III of the Constitution: Article III, Section 1 [636] vests the judicial power of the United States in the "Supreme Court and in such inferior courts as the Congress may from time to time ordain and establish" and Article III, Section 2 [637] then delineates that power. Article III does not confer subject matter jurisdiction upon federal courts other than the Supreme Court. Rather, the power to confer subject matter jurisdiction is given to Congress, which has done so through the "enabling statutes," *e.g.,* 28 U.S.C. §§ 1330–1369 [15] and 28 U.S.C. §§ 1441–

1452 [28]. The most common sources of federal
subject matter jurisdiction encountered in the first
year of law school are (1) federal question
jurisdiction—where the action arises under federal
law, 28 U.S.C. § 1331 [16], and (2) diversity of
citizenship jurisdiction, where the action is between
citizens of different states and the amount in
controversy is, currently, more than $75,000, 28
U.S.C. § 1332 [17].

Federal question jurisdiction exists for "civil
actions *arising under* the Constitution, laws, or
treaties of the United States." 28 U.S.C. § 1331 [16]
(emphasis added). To meet the "arising under"
requirement of §1331, it is not enough that a federal
law might be implicated or provide a defense to the
action. Rather, federal question jurisdiction extends
over "only those cases in which a well-pleaded
complaint establishes either that federal law creates
the cause of action or that the plaintiff's right to
relief necessarily depends on resolution of a
substantial question of federal law," *Franchise Tax
Board of California v. Construction Laborers
Vacation Trust*, 463 U.S. 1, 27–28 (1983) [96], in
that "federal law is a necessary element of one of the
well-pleaded . . . claims," *id.* at 13 [95]. Thus, with
only a few exceptions, the federal question must be
rooted in the allegations of the complaint itself.

Even if federal question jurisdiction is absent,
federal courts may hear actions based on diversity of
citizenship jurisdiction under 28 U.S.C. § 1332 [17].
Diversity jurisdiction is based on the identity of the
parties and generally is determined at the time the

action is filed.   There are two essential
requirements:

> (1) Complete diversity—meaning no plaintiff
> may be a citizen of the same state as any of
> the defendants, *Strawbridge v. Curtiss*, 7
> U.S. (3 Cranch) 267 (1806) [74];[1] and
>
> (2) The amount in controversy must exceed
> $75,000.[2]

A motion under Rule 12(b)(1) [181] may be
brought by any party at any time in the
proceedings. Further, if the court determines at any
time that it lacks subject matter jurisdiction, it
must dismiss the action.   FED. R. CIV. P.
12(h)(3) [192].   Hence, a defense based on lack of
federal subject matter jurisdiction is never waived
and, you will recall, subject matter jurisdiction

---

[1] Individuals are considered citizens of the state in which they
are "domiciled," that is, the most recent state where they resided
and intended to remain.   Corporations are considered citizens of
both the state where they were incorporated and the state of
their principal place of business—the place "where [the]
corporation's high level officers direct, control, and coordinate the
corporation's activities" in other words, their "'nerve center.'"
Hertz Corp. v. Friend, 130 S. Ct. 1181, 1186 (2010) [1].   There are
exceptions to the requirement of complete diversity, for example,
in class actions and multi-district litigation.

[2] The minimum amount in controversy required for diversity
jurisdiction is an additional requirement imposed by Congress
and is not part of Article 3.   The threshold amount has steadily
increased over the years and currently must exceed $75,000.   To
justify dismissal based on failure to meet the minimum amount
in controversy "[i]t must appear to a legal certainty that the
claim is really for less than the jurisdictional amount . . . ." *St.
Paul Mercury Indem. Co. v. Red Cab Co.*, 303 U.S. 283, 289
(1938) [75].

cannot be conferred by agreement or the consent of the parties.

QUESTIONS

1. Are there grounds for a Rule 12(b)(1) [181] motion in *Neely v. Fox*? Why or why not?

2. Why, in general, might a defendant want to bring a 12(b)(1) [181] motion?

C.   RULE 12(b)(2)—LACK OF PERSONAL JURISDICTION

1. Overview

Motions under 12(b)(2) [182] are based on lack of personal jurisdiction. A court must also have personal jurisdiction over the parties in the case so that it has the power to render a judgment against them. This will depend on a party's connection with the state in which the action is filed (known as the "forum state"). That connection must be great enough to give a court in the forum state the power to enter a binding order or judgment against the party. A court's power to exercise personal jurisdiction over a party is limited by the applicable state personal jurisdiction statute, known as the "long-arm statute," and the due process clauses [635] of the Constitution. Personal jurisdiction has a few more details and hurdles than subject matter jurisdiction, as will be evident in the brief overview provided below.

2. State Long Arm Statutes

States may prescribe the jurisdictional limits of courts within their boundaries by statute. A state's long arm statute cannot provide for the exercise of personal jurisdiction beyond constitutional limits, and many states' long arm statutes simply provide that courts may exercise jurisdiction over individuals and corporations up to the limits of the Due Process Clause. *See, e.g.*, Ark. Code. Ann. § 16–4–101 [129]; Cal. Code Civ. Proc. § 410.10 [143]; Nev. Rev. Stat. § 14.065 [475]. Other state long arm statutes provide for the exercise of personal jurisdiction in more limited circumstances, however. *See, e.g.*, Mass. Gen. Laws Ann. ch. 223A § 3 [394]; N.Y.C.P.L.R. § 302 [477]. Thus it is important to first consult the long arm statute of the forum state when considering whether to file a motion to dismiss for lack of personal jurisdiction—or where to file a complaint in the first place.

3. Due Process Requirements

i. Overview

For a court to exercise personal jurisdiction over a defendant, due process requires first that the defendant have received adequate notice of the action. (Notice is discussed in subsection (f)(2), p. 39, below). Next, the defendant must either:

- be present in the forum state when the action is commenced; be a citizen of the forum state; or have its principal place of business in that state;

- have consented to personal jurisdiction by courts in the forum state, either expressly, impliedly, or through waiver; or

- have sufficient minimum contacts with the forum state.

If, after adequate notice, any of these conditions is satisfied, the exercise of personal jurisdiction by a court in the forum state is proper under the Constitution. *McIntyre Machinery, Ltd. v. Nicastro*, 131 S. Ct. 2780, 2787 (2011) [2].

ii. General vs. Specific Personal Jurisdiction

There are two types of personal jurisdiction: "general or all-purpose jurisdiction and specific or case-linked jurisdiction." *Goodyear Dunlop Tires Operations, S.A. v. Brown*, 131 S. Ct. 2846, 2851 (2011) [5]. A court with general jurisdiction over a party may hear and decide claims against a party that are unrelated to the party's activities in the forum state.[3] A court with specific jurisdiction may

---

[3] Of the methods of obtaining personal jurisdiction that are set out above, the first three, a party's presence, citizenship, or consent, will allow the exercise of general personal jurisdiction over that party. *McIntyre Machinery, Ltd. v. Nicastro*, 131 S. Ct. 2780, 2787 (2011) [2]. If not, "a party's affiliations with the State [must be] so 'continuous and systematic' as to render them essentially at home in the forum State." *Goodyear Dunlop Tires Operations, S.A. v. Brown*, 131 S.Ct. 2846, 2851 (2011) [5] (quoting *International Shoe Co. v. Washington*, 326 U.S. 310, 317 (1945) [80]). For example, in *Perkins v. Benguet Consol. Mining Co.*, 342 U.S. 437, 447–48 (1952) [84], the defendant, a Philippine mining corporation, ceased activities in the Philippines during World War II. During that time its affairs were overseen in Ohio—where its president maintained his office, kept the company files, and supervised company activities. The Ohio

only hear and decide claims that "arise out of or are connected with the [party's] activities within the state." *International Shoe Co. v. Washington*, 326 U.S. 310, 319 (1945) [81]. Thus, specific personal jurisdiction is sometime referred to as "arising out of" jurisdiction.[4]

4. Presence

Personal jurisdiction in the forum state can be established if an individual is personally served with a summons while he or she is physically within the boundaries of that state, even if the individual is there only temporarily and for reasons unrelated to the suit. *Burnham v. Superior Court of Cal. County of Marin*, 495 U.S. 604, 612–22 (1990) [106]. In *Burnham*, for example, a California court acquired personal jurisdiction in a divorce proceeding over a New Jersey resident when he was served with

---

court properly exercised general jurisdiction over the defendant because "Ohio was [its] principal, if temporary, place of business." *Keeton v. Hustler Magazine, Inc.*, 465 U.S. 770, 779–780, n. 11 (1984) [98].

[4] If the action "arises out of or relates to" a party's affiliation with the forum state, courts in that state may exercise specific jurisdiction over it if the party has "certain minimum contacts with [the forum State] such that the maintenance of the suit does not offend traditional notions of fair play and substantial justice." *International Shoe Co. v. Washington*, 326 U.S. 310, 316 (1945) [79] (internal quotations omitted). The majority of personal jurisdiction cases you will read in the first year of law school involve specific jurisdiction. *See Goodyear Dunlop Tires Operations, S.A. v. Brown*, 131 S.Ct. 2846, 2854 (2011) [6] (where the Court points out that "specific jurisdiction has become the centerpiece of modern jurisdiction theory, while general jurisdiction plays a reduced role").

summons while in California on an unrelated business trip.

5. Citizenship

Personal jurisdiction may also be exercised over individuals who are citizens of the forum state, meaning they are domiciled there, and "by analogy," to corporations who are incorporated or have their principal place of business in the forum state. *McIntyre Machinery, Ltd. v. Nicastro*, 131 S. Ct. 2780, 2787 (2011) [2]. Generally, an individual is considered to be domiciled in the state where they reside and intend to remain. A corporation's principal place of business is where its "nerve center" is located—"where the corporation's high level officers direct, control, and coordinate the corporation's activities." *Hertz Corp. v. Friend*, 130 S. Ct. 1181, 1186 (2010) [1] (indicating "that the 'nerve center' will typically be found at a corporation's headquarters").

6. Consent or Waiver

Unlike subject matter jurisdiction, personal jurisdiction *can* be expressly or impliedly consented to or acquired through waiver. Parties may expressly consent to personal jurisdiction, for example, by voluntarily appearing before a court and submitting to its jurisdiction. Or parties to a contract may expressly consent in advance to submit to the jurisdiction of a particular court through a "forum selection clause" in a contract.[5]

7. Minimum Contacts

The basic and oft-stated rule is that a state may authorize its courts to exercise jurisdiction over an out-of-state defendant if the defendant has "certain minimum contacts with [the state] such that the maintenance of the suit does not offend traditional notions of fair play and substantial justice." *International Shoe Co. v. Washington*, 326 U.S. 310, 316 (1945) [79] (internal quotations omitted). In making this determination, courts generally focus on "the relationship among the defendant, the forum, and the litigation." *Shaffer v. Heitner*, 433 U.S. 186, 204 (1977) [89].

Since the *International Shoe* case, many Supreme Court decisions have elaborated on the circumstances under which a court may exercise jurisdiction based on minimum contacts. As a general rule, though, the Court has looked to whether there was "some act by which the defendant *purposefully avail[ed]* itself of the privilege of conducting activities within the forum State, thus invoking the benefits and protections of

---

[5] Courts have found implied consent to personal jurisdiction when a party initiates suit in a particular court—meaning that court acquires jurisdiction to enter judgment against a party on a counter claim made by the defendant. Personal jurisdiction may also be acquired through waiver if the defense of lack of personal jurisdiction is not timely raised in a motion to dismiss or in the answer to the complaint. *See Insurance Corp. of Ireland, Ltd. v. Compagnie des Bauxites de Guinee*, 456 U.S. 694 (1982) [94].

its laws." *Goodyear Dunlop Tires Operations, S.A. v. Brown*, 131 S.Ct. 2846, 2854 (2011) [6] (emphasis added) (quoting *Hanson v. Denckla*, 357 U.S. 235, 253 (1958) [85]). In some cases this inquiry involves determining whether there was an action by the defendant that was "*purposely directed* toward the forum state." *Asahi Metal Industry Co. v. Superior Court of Cal., Solano Cty.*, 480 U.S. 102, 112 (1987) [104] (emphasis added).[6]

---

[6] In essence, the defendant's contacts or connection with the forum state must be purposeful as opposed to merely conceivable. For example, in *Asahi*, a Taiwanese tire manufacturer settled a product liability action brought in California and brought an indemnification action in California against a Japanese valve assembly manufacturer that had placed its valves in the "stream of commerce." The Court held that the Japanese company's "mere awareness . . . that the components it manufactured, sold, and delivered outside the United States would reach the forum State in the stream of commerce" was insufficient to permit the exercise of jurisdiction by the California court. *Asahi Metal Industry Co. v. Superior Court of Cal., Solano Cty.* 480 U.S. 102, 109 (1987) [103]. In *World–Wide Volkswagen Corp. v. Woodson*, 444 U.S. 286, 287, 297 (1980) [92], the Court held that an Oklahoma court could not exercise personal jurisdiction "over a nonresident automobile retailer and its wholesale distributor in a products-liability action, when the defendants' only connection with Oklahoma is the fact that an automobile sold in New York to New York residents became involved in an accident in Oklahoma." On the other hand, in *Burger King Corp. v. Rudzewicz*, 471 U.S. 462, 474–475 (1985) [99], the Court held that a Florida court could exercise jurisdiction in a breach of contract action brought by a franchisor headquartered in Florida against Michigan franchisees, because the franchise agreement called for long-term and on-going interactions between the franchisees and the franchisor's Florida headquarters. In that case, the Court determined that the franchisee had "purposely established minimum contacts with the forum State." *Id.* at 476 [100].

8. Procedure

A defense based on lack of personal jurisdiction may be asserted in a motion under Rule 12(b)(2) [182] or in the answer to the complaint. If the defense is asserted by a Rule 12(b)(2) motion, the motion must be filed before the answer. *See* FED. R. CIV. P. 12(b) [182] ("A motion making any of these defenses shall be made before pleading if a further pleading is permitted."). Failure to assert the defense by motion or in the answer or amended answer will usually result in waiver, i.e., submission to the court's jurisdiction. *See* Fed. R. Civ. P. 12(h) [191]. Indeed, many jurisdictions require a party challenging personal jurisdiction to file a "special appearance" before or at the same time as the motion or answer—otherwise the defense is waived. Essentially, a "special appearance" is a way of appearing and thus consenting to personal jurisdiction for the sole and limited purpose of challenging personal jurisdiction and having the court rule on that challenge.

Once a motion to dismiss for lack of personal jurisdiction under Rule 12(b)(2) [182] is brought, the plaintiff has the burden of establishing sufficient jurisdictional facts. Courts will consider extrinsic evidence outside the pleadings and generally will decide motions challenging jurisdiction before other dispositive motions.

QUESTIONS

1. Are there grounds for a Rule 12(b)(2) [182] motion in *Neely v. Fox*? Why or why not?

2. Did the United States District Court for the Eastern District of Tennessee have personal jurisdiction over Fox of Oak Ridge, Inc.?

3. If yes, based on what grounds?

4. What are the differences between general and specific personal jurisdiction?

5. Was the court's personal jurisdiction over Fox of Oak Ridge, Inc. general or specific? Explain.

6. Did the United States District Court for the Eastern District of Tennessee have personal jurisdiction over Benjamin Curd?

7. If yes, based on what grounds?

8. Was the court's personal jurisdiction over Benjamin Curd general or specific? Explain.

9. Tennessee's long arm statute is TENN. CODE ANN. § 20–2–225 [494]. Is it more restrictive than the limits of the U.S. Constitution? Why or why not?

D.   RULE 12(b)(3)—IMPROPER VENUE

While the question of personal jurisdiction "goes to the court's power to exercise control over the parties, . . . venue . . . is primarily a matter of choosing a convenient forum." *Leroy v. Great Western United Corp.*, 443 U.S. 173, 180 [91] (1979). Motions to dismiss for improper venue under Rule 12(b)(3) [184] challenge whether the action was brought in the right location, i.e., district.   The general statute governing venue in federal courts is 28 U.S.C. § 1391 [25], which provides that venue is proper in the district in which:

(1) any defendant resides, if all defendants are residents of the State in which the district is located;

(2) a substantial part of the events or omissions giving rise to the action occurred; or

(3) a substantial part of the property at issue in the action is located.

Parties may also consent to venue in a particular district by waiving a valid objection to venue after an action is commenced. In addition, many contracts contain "forum selection clauses" in which the parties agree that disputes involving the contract will be heard in a specific venue. A defense based on improper venue may be asserted in the answer to the complaint or in a Rule 12(b)(3) [184] motion filed before the answer. A motion under Rule 12(b)(3) [184] is also the proper method of enforcing a forum selection clause in a contract. Once a defendant brings a Rule 12(b)(3) [184] motion, the plaintiff has the burden of showing that venue is proper, and courts may consider evidence outside the pleadings in ruling on the motion.

QUESTIONS

1. What paragraphs of the complaint in *Neely v. Fox* contain allegations concerning venue?

2. Here [643] is a map showing all the districts in the federal system, and here is a map of the counties in Tennessee [642]. Based on your review of the pertinent allegations in the complaint and the maps:

a. Are there grounds for a Rule 12(b)(3) [184] motion in *Neely v. Fox*? Why or why not?

b. Was venue proper in the United States District Court for the Eastern District of Tennessee, Northern Division?

c. If yes, based on what grounds?

E.   RULE 12(b)(4)—INSUFFICIENT PROCESS

Motions to dismiss under Rule 12(b)(4) [185] challenge the form or contents of the summons and are based on noncompliance with Federal Rule of Civil Procedure 4(a) [311], which governs a summons' contents. For example, a summons that fails to set out the proper names of the parties or the court would be defective under Rule 4(a)(1)(A) [312]. Dismissals based on mere technical defects in the summons are disfavored, however.   Thus, defendants bringing Rule 12(b)(4) [185] motions will generally have to show (1) actual prejudice, e.g., that the defects in the summons were so numerous or pronounced that the defendants did not know they were being sued, *see U.S.A. Nutrasource, Inc. v. CAN Ins. Co.*, 140 F.Supp.2d 1049, 1052 (N.D. Cal. 2001) [7], or (2) that the plaintiff made virtually no attempt to comply with Rule 4, *see, e.g., Wasson v. Riverside County*, 237 F.R.D. 423, 424 (C.D. Cal. 2006) [10] (summons and complaint did not name the purported defendant).

QUESTIONS

Please review (1) the summonses (Fox of Oak Ridge [430] and Curd [440]) filed in *Neely v. Fox*, (2) Rule 4(a) [311], and (3) Rule 12(a) [179], and answer the following:

1. Are there any errors or defects in either of the summonses?

2. If there are errors do you think they would have formed the grounds for a successful motion to dismiss under Rule 12(b)(4) [185]?

F. RULE 12(b)(5)—INSUFFICIENT SERVICE OF PROCESS

1. Overview

While a Rule 12(b)(4) [185] motion challenges the contents of the summons itself, a motion for insufficient service of process under Rule 12(b)(5) [186] challenges the method or manner in which the summons and complaint were served or whether they were served at all. The requirements for service of process are set out in Rule 4 [289]. In general, Rule 4(c) [313] provides that "[a] summons must be served with a copy of the complaint" and that "[t]he plaintiff is responsible for having the summons and complaint served within the time allowed by Rule 4(m) [322]—usually 120 days from when the complaint is filed. Rule 4(c) [313] also specifies who may make service—generally "[a]ny person who is at least 18 years old and not a party. . . ."

Requirements for service of process must be met in order for a district court to acquire personal jurisdiction over an individual or entity. *See* Fed. R. Civ. P. 4(k) [320]. As the court in *Mann v. Castiel*, 681 F.3d 368, 372 (D.C. Cir. 2012) [116], explained:

> Service is . . . not only a means of notifying a defendant of the commencement of an action against him, but a ritual that marks the court's assertion of jurisdiction over the lawsuit. Consequently, courts have uniformly held . . . a judgment is void where the requirements for effective service have not been satisfied.

2. Service of Process on Individuals

Rule 4(e) [315] governs service of process on individuals within the United States. The three basic methods of service are

(1) personal service,

(2) substitute or substituted service, and

(3) service by publication, sometimes referred to as "constructive service."

As explained in Chapter 2, ideally, the summons and complaint are served directly, that is, given by the plaintiff to the defendant personally. This method is most likely to afford actual notice and greatly reduces the likelihood that service of process will be challenged. Rule 4(e)(2)(B) [317], however, also authorizes substitute service, which is accomplished by "leaving a copy of [the summons and complaint] at the individual's dwelling or usual place of abode with someone of suitable age and discretion who resides there."

Furthermore, Rule 4(e)(1) [316] provides that service may be made under the procedures allowed by the law of the state in which the federal district court is located or service is made. Thus, although Rule 4 [289] does not contain a specific provision regarding service by publication, many states provide for this manner of service under specified conditions. *See, e.g.*, N.C. R. CIV. P. 4(j)(1) [400]; UTAH R. CIV. P. 4(d)(4) [638]. Many states also allow for service by mail or commercial courier service, provided the defendant signs an acknowledgement of receipt. *See, e.g.*, N.C. R. CIV. P. 4(j)(1)(c) [401]; UTAH R. CIV. P. 4(d)(2) [639].

Due Process—Notice: Service by publication or other means under state law must comport with Constitutional due process in order for a district court to acquire personal jurisdiction over a defendant. Due process requires adequate notice and an opportunity to be heard—which means "notice reasonably calculated, under all the circumstances, to apprise interested parties of the pendency of the action and afford them an opportunity to present their objections." *Mullane v. Central Hanover Bank & Trust Co.*, 339 U.S. 306, 314 (1950) [83]. Thus, all methods of service of process authorized by state law must comport with this standard.

3. Service of Process on Corporations, Partnerships, and Associations

Rule 4(h) [318] governs service of process on corporations, partnerships, and associations. It allows for service of process authorized by state law under Rule 4(e)(1) [316]—subject to due process requirements. In addition, Rule 4(h)(1)(b) [319] authorizes service:

> by delivering a copy of the summons and of the complaint to an officer, a managing or general agent, or any other agent authorized by appointment or by law to receive service of process and—if the agent is one authorized by statute and the statute so requires—by also mailing a copy of each to the defendant. . . .

Note that most states require corporations and other business associations doing business in the state to appoint an authorized agent for accepting service of process.

4. Challenging Service of Process

In many instances, challenges to service of process are made in a motion for relief from judgment under Federal Rule of Civil Procedure 60(b)(4) [349] on grounds that the judgment is void. This is because requirements for service of process must be satisfied for a district court to acquire personal jurisdiction over defendants and judgments entered by a court without personal jurisdiction are void. *Mann v. Castiel*, 681 F.3d 368, 372 [116] (D.C. Cir. 2012). In these cases, the moving party usually has learned of the action only after judgment has been entered, and the basis of their Rule 60 [345] motion is service of process was insufficient and did not afford them with adequate notice.

In contrast, a motion to dismiss for insufficient service of process under Rule 12(b)(5) [186] is filed prior to the entry of judgment, before or in lieu of filing an answer. At this early stage of a case, requirements under Rule 4 [289] are generally to be construed in favor of upholding service as long as the defendant had sufficient notice of the action. *Chan v. Society Expeditions, Inc.*, 39 F.3d 1398, 1404 (9th Cir. 1994) [86]. Thus, as with Rule 12(b)(4) [185] motions to dismiss for insufficient process, motions to dismiss under Rule 12(b)(5) [186] based on mere technical defects in service are not likely to be successful. The moving party will need to show actual prejudice, which is rare in cases where the defendant had sufficient notice of the action to bring the Rule 12(b)(4) motion in the first place, or show that the plaintiff made no attempt to properly serve them with the summons and complaint. *See, e.g., Mann v. Castiel*, 681 F.3d 368, 373 (D.C. Cir. 2012) [393] (although the movants were aware of the lawsuit, "[p]laintiffs offered no evidence to the district court to show that the three defendants had been served, much less properly served"); *Wasson v. Riverside County*, 237 F.R.D. 423, 424 (C.D. Cal. 2006) [10] (school district was merely mailed a copy of the complaint; it was not named in the complaint, nor had a summons naming it been issued or served on it).

Note also that dismissals for insufficient service
of process under Rule 12(b)(5) [186] are generally
"without prejudice," *see* Rule 4(m) [322], meaning
the plaintiff may file another complaint and
reattempt service as long as the applicable statutes
of limitation have not run. Thus, even if the
plaintiff did not properly comply with the
requirements for service of process, defense counsel
should be circumspect in filing a motion to dismiss
under Rule 12(b)(5) [186] unless the plaintiff's
failure to comply was egregious and a good
argument can be made that the applicable statutes
of limitation have run.

QUESTIONS

1. Did either Fox of Oak Ridge or Benjamin Curd
   have grounds to bring a motion to dismiss under
   Rule 12(b)(5) [186]? Why or why not?

2. Look up the rule or rules regarding service of
   process in your state.

   a. Does your state authorize any methods of
      service of process that are not specifically
      described in Federal Rule of Civil Procedure
      4 [289]?

   b. If yes, what additional methods are
      authorized?

   c. Do you think these additional methods
      comport with the "reasonably calculated to
      . . . apprise" standard set out in *Mullane v.
      Central Hanover Bank & Trust Co.*, 339 U.S.
      306, 314 (1950) [83].

G.   RULE 12(b)(6)—FAILURE TO STATE A CLAIM UPON WHICH RELIEF CAN BE GRANTED

1. Overview

A motion to dismiss under Rule 12(b)(6) [187] challenges the sufficiency of the claims in the complaint. It is the only motion under Rule 12(b) [180] that attacks the complaint on substantive grounds. As explained in Chapter 2, section VI, Rule 8(a)(2) [364], p. 13 requires a complaint to contain a "short and plain statement of the claim showing that the pleader is entitled to relief." In a Rule 12(b)(6) [187] motion to dismiss the defendant's position is: even if the factual allegations in the complaint are taken as true, the plaintiff is not entitled to relief. A successful motion disposes of a claim early on—before having to go through the expense of discovery. A quality Rule 12(b)(6) [187] motion, even if denied, may also educate and make an impression on the judge regarding weaknesses in the plaintiff's case. However, the same motion is likely to educate the plaintiff as well and cause counsel to amend the complaint with better or better-stated claims.

2. Materials Considered in Deciding a Rule 12(b)(6) Motion

A court may not consider extrinsic evidence—matters outside the pleadings—in deciding a motion to dismiss under Rule 12(b)(6) [187]. If a party does submit extrinsic evidence, and that evidence is not excluded by the court, "the motion must be treated as a motion for summary judgment under Rule 56 [334]." Fed. R. Civ. P. 12(d) [190]. If a Rule 12(b)(6) [187] motion is converted into a motion for summary judgment, "All parties must be given a reasonable opportunity to present all the material that is pertinent to the motion," Rule 12(d) [190], and afforded time to conduct discovery, Rule 56(f) [340].

Matters within the pleadings include the allegations in the complaint, as well as any documents attached as exhibits to the complaint. *See* Fed. R. Civ. P. 10(c) [174]. Also, a court may consider matters of public record, *Ennenga v. Starns*, 677 F.3d 766, 774–75 (7th Cir. 2012) [115], as well as documents incorporated by reference in the complaint, or those referred to, or relied on in the complaint as long as "the document is central to the plaintiff's claim, and no party questions the authenticity of the document" *Sanders v. Brown*, 504 F.3d 903, 910 (9th Cir. 2007) [108].

3. The Standard Applied in Deciding a Motion to Dismiss

"To survive a motion to dismiss [under rule 12(b)(6) [187]], a complaint must contain sufficient factual matter, that, if accepted as true, 'state[s] a claim to relief that is plausible on its face.'" *Ashcroft v. Iqbal*, 556 U.S. 662, 678 (2009) [111] (quoting *Bell Atlantic Corp. v. Twombly*, 550 U.S. 544, 570 (2007) [110]). This standard creates a two-step process in deciding a Rule 12(b)(6) [187] motion. First, the court will parse out, and not accept as true, allegations that amount to legal conclusions. "Hence, [t]hreadbare recitals of the elements of a cause of action, supported by mere conclusory statements, do not suffice." *Ashcroft v. Iqbal*, 556 U.S. at 678 [111]. Thus, for example, in a personal injury claim based on negligence, it is not enough to simply allege the defendant "acted negligently and without due care and that such negligence proximately caused the plaintiff's injuries."

Second, the court will determine whether "the well-pleaded, nonconclusory factual allegation[s]" state "a plausible claim for relief." *Ashcroft v. Iqbal*, 556 U.S. at 679–80 [133]. Plausible means more than merely conceivable and requires "more than a sheer possibility that a defendant has acted unlawfully." *Id.* at 678 [131]. Rather, "[a] claim has facial plausibility when the plaintiff pleads factual content that allows the court to draw the reasonable inference that the defendant is liable for the misconduct alleged."[7] *Id.* [131]

---

[7] In *Ashcroft v. Iqbal* [136], the Supreme Court considered whether the factual allegation that government officials "arrested and detained thousands of Arab-Muslim men . . . as part of its investigation of the events of September 11[, 2001]" plausibly suggested an entitlement to relief for invidious discrimination, and held it did not. Specifically, the Court noted the September 11 attacks were perpetrated by 19 Arab-Muslim men, and "[i]t should come as no surprise that a legitimate policy directing law enforcement to arrest and detain individuals because of their suspected link to the attacks would produce a disparate, incidental impact on Arab-Muslims, even though the purpose of the policy was to target neither Arabs nor Muslims." *Id.* at 682 [135]. The court stated, "As between that obvious alternative explanation for the arrests . . . and the purposeful, invidious discrimination respondent asks us to infer, discrimination is not

4. Considerations in Filing a Rule 12(b)(6) Motion to Dismiss

Generally, counsel should consider filing a Rule 12(b)(6) [187] motion to dismiss when the complaint has these types of defects: First, if the allegations are conclusory and merely parrot the legal elements of a claim without specific factual details in support. A motion to dismiss in these circumstances may expose the claim as wholly unsubstantiated and frivolous, or it may force the plaintiff to show the specific facts she is relying on to support her claims. On the other hand, if the factual allegations are arguably sufficiently detailed, a Rule 12(b)(6) [187] motion to dismiss may be a needless expenditure of the client's and court's resources.

Second, if the factual allegations, even if adequately detailed, fail to support the claim. This may be because an essential element is missing; for example, if the claim is for assault and battery and there are no allegations that the defendant acted intentionally. Or the plaintiff's claim may be based on a statute that was not in effect at the time of the injury or dispute. Finally, the factual allegations may present a claim that is merely conceivable, but not plausible given an obvious alternative lawful

---

a plausible conclusion." *Id.* [135] Accordingly, the Court held the claimant had "not 'nudged [his] claims' of invidious discrimination 'across the line from conceivable to plausible.'" *Id.* at 681 [134] (quoting *Bell Atlantic Corp. v. Twombly*, 550 U.S. 544, 570 (2007) [110].

explanation. *See Ashcroft v. Iqbal*, 556 U.S. 662, 678 (2009) [111].

Third, the factual allegations in the complaint may adequately state a claim for relief in themselves, but this claim is foreclosed by an affirmative defense—for example, the statute of limitations applicable to the claim has run or the defendant is immune from suit. Before filing a motion to dismiss based on an affirmative defense, counsel should evaluate whether proving the defense would require consideration of extrinsic evidence—matters outside the pleadings. If this is a real possibility, a motion for summary judgment would probably be more appropriate.

In any of these three situations, counsel should weigh the costs versus the potential benefits before filing a motion to dismiss under Rule 12(b)(6) [187]. A motion that would likely curtail or streamline the litigation—by eliminating claims or forcing the plaintiff to set out the specific facts upon which his claims are based—is a prudent step. On the other hand, a motion that merely vexes while at the same time educates the plaintiff or that is likely to depend on matters outside the pleadings is often not a good use of time and expense.

QUESTIONS

Review the complaint [407] filed in *Neely v. Fox* and answer the following:

    1.   What claims are alleged?

2. On what theory are the claims against Fox of Oak Ridge based?

3. Review the allegations supporting each claim. Do you think any of these allegations are conclusory under *Ashcroft v. Iqbal*, 556 U.S. at 678 [111]? If yes, which ones and why do you think they are conclusory?

4. If you think that any of the allegations supporting plaintiff claims are conclusory, do you think they would warrant a motion to dismiss under 12(b)(6) [187]?

5. Do you think the factual allegations in the complaint meet the "plausible claim for relief" standard explained in *Ashcroft v. Iqbal*, 556 U.S. at 678–80 [111]?

6. Can you think of any affirmative defenses that might support a motion to dismiss for failure to state a claim under Rule 12(b)(6) [187]?

H.   RULE 12(b)(7)—FAILURE TO JOIN AN INDISPENSABLE PARTY UNDER RULE 19

1. Overview

A motion under Rule 12(b)(7) [188] allows an action to be dismissed for the plaintiff's failure to join an indispensable party under Rule 19 [211]. Rule 19 [211] governs permissive and mandatory joinder of parties and requires a three-part analysis to determine whether an absent party is "indispensable." If the absent party is ruled indispensable, the action must be dismissed. The court must decide:

(1) whether the absent party is a "required" or "necessary"[8] party;

(2) if so, whether it is possible for that party to be joined; and

(3) if joinder of a party is not possible, whether that party is indispensable—that is "whether, in equity and good conscience, the action should proceed among the existing parties or should be dismissed." Fed. R. Civ. P. 19(a) & (b) [212].

A defendant will usually file a motion to dismiss under Rule 12(b)(7) [188] when (1) the plaintiff has deliberately failed to join a party because the court lacks personal jurisdiction over that party or where joining the party would destroy federal subject matter diversity jurisdiction, or (2) where a named party has been dismissed based on the lack of personal or subject matter jurisdiction. The court may consider extrinsic evidence in deciding the motion.

2. Required or Necessary Parties

Under Rule 19(a)(1) [213], a person[9] is a required or necessary party if:

---

[8] Fed. R. Civ. P. 19 [211] now uses the term "required" instead of "necessary," but many courts continue to use the term "necessary."

[9] "Person" is a broad legal term and includes artificial entities such as corporations. When statutes, rules, or courts are referring only to humans they will often use the term "individual"

(A) in that person's absence, the court cannot accord complete relief among existing parties; or

(B) that person claims an interest relating to the subject of the action and is so situated that disposing of the action in the person's absence may:

(i) as a practical matter impair or impede the person's ability to protect the interest; or

(ii) leave an existing party subject to a substantial risk of incurring double, multiple, or otherwise inconsistent obligations because of the interest.

The first category of required or necessary parties—those in whose absence complete relief cannot be afforded to the plaintiff—is relatively narrow and does not include tortfeasors who are jointly and severally liable along with the named defendant. It is not necessary for all joint tortfeasors to be named in a single lawsuit because, although more than one person may be responsible for the plaintiff's damages, it is possible for the plaintiff to obtain complete relief from fewer than all of them. *Temple v. Synthes Corp., Ltd.*, 498 U.S. 5, 7–8 [502] (1990) (in products liability action against manufacturer of a plate and screw device that was implanted in patient's lower spine, the doctor who performed the surgery and hospital in which it was performed were not necessary parties

---

or "natural person." *See Mohammad v. Palestinian Authority*, 132 S.Ct. 1702, 1706–07 (2012) [396].

under Rule 19 [211]). However, if the absent party has control over whether or how the requested relief will be effectuated, that party will be considered required or necessary under Rule 19(a)(1)(A) [213]. *See, e.g., City of Syracuse v. Onondaga County*, 464 F.3d 297, 299 (2nd Cir. 2006) [97] (the city was a necessary party in environmental action against Onondaga County where an injunction required the county to construct a sewage treatment facility within city limits and approval of the city to purchase the property on which to build the facility was required).

The second category of required or necessary parties—those who claim a sufficient interest in the subject matter of the lawsuit—is broader. Typically a necessary party under this second category (1) is a party to a contract that is the subject of the litigation or a joint title holder in property that is the subject of the litigation, and (2) the litigation will result in a judgment that will affect the absent party's rights under or to the contract or property. *See Dawavendewa v. Salt River Project Agric. Improvement & Power Dist.*, 276 F.3d 1150, 1156–57 (9th Cir. 2002) [11] (where plaintiff's action challenged a hiring preference called for in a lease between the defendant and an Indian tribe, the tribe was a necessary party under Rule 19(a)(2) [215] because it "claim[ed] a legally protected interest in its contract rights with [the defendant].")

3. Whether Joinder of a Required or Necessary Party is Possible

If an absent party is required or necessary, that party must be joined if possible. Joinder of a party is not feasible however, if (1) the court would then lack subject matter jurisdiction over the claim because joining the party would destroy diversity, *see* 28 U.S.C. § 1332 [17]; (2) the court lacks subject matter over the absent party, *see McIntyre Machinery, Ltd. v. Nicastro*, 131 S.Ct. 2780, 2787 (2011) [2]; or (3) the absent party has sovereign immunity and thus is not susceptible to suit absent an express waiver; *Dawavendewa v. Salt River Project Agric. Improvement & Power Dist.*, 276 F.3d 1150, 1159 (9th Cir. 2002) [12]. If joinder is not possible, the court then determines if the absent party is indispensable.

4. Whether the Absent Party is Indispensable

In determining whether a required or necessary party is indispensable, a court must decide whether "in equity and good conscience, the action should proceed among the existing parties or should be dismissed." Fed. R. Civ. P. 19(b). The court must consider these four factors:

    (1) the extent to which a judgment rendered in the person's absence might prejudice that person or the existing parties;

    (2) the extent to which any prejudice could be lessened or avoided by:

        (a) protective provisions in the judgment;

    (b) shaping the relief; or

    (c) other measures;

(3) whether a judgment rendered in the person's absence would be adequate; and

(4) whether the plaintiff would have an adequate remedy if the action were dismissed for nonjoinder. Fed. R. Civ. P. 19(b) [216].

In essence, when determining indispensability, the court must weigh and balance the rights and interests of the absent party, the plaintiff, and existing parties and determine the impact on those rights of the action going forward versus being dismissed. *Provident Tradesmen Bank & Trust Co. v. Patterson*, 390 U.S. 102, 118–19 (1968) [87]; *HB General Corp. v. Manchester Partners, L.P.*, 95 F.3d 1185, 1190–93 (3rd Cir. 1996) [126] (where all three partners of a small limited partnership were before the court, the court determined that the partnership, which could not be joined without destroying diversity jurisdiction, was not an indispensable party).

QUESTIONS

1. Can you think of any person not named in the complaint who might be an indispensable party in *Neely v. Fox*?

2. If the plaintiff had sued only Fox of Oak Ridge, would Benjamin Curd have been an indispensable party? Why or why not?

3. What if the plaintiff had sued only Benjamin
    Curd? Would Fox of Oak Ridge have been an
    indispensable party? Why or why not?

III. RESPONDING BY AN ANSWER
TO THE COMPLAINT

A. OVERVIEW

Defendants frequently respond to the complaint
by filing an answer rather than a motion to dismiss,
as was the case in *Neely v. Fox.* While the plaintiff
can use the complaint to initially frame the issues in
the case to its advantage, the answer is the
defendant's opportunity to frame the issues from its
perspective. The form and contents of the answer
are governed by court or procedural rules. In
federal cases the defendant must:

(1) admit or deny the allegations in the
    complaint;

(2) set out any affirmative defenses, and

(3) state any compulsory counterclaims the
    defendant has against the plaintiff.

Fed. R. Civ. P. 8(b) & (c) [365]; Fed. R. Civ. P. 13(a)
[194]. The answer may also set out any non-
compulsory counterclaims against the plaintiff as
well as any cross-claims against co-defendants. By
filing the answer, counsel is certifying that the
defenses, claims, and contentions therein are not
frivolous and that the contentions and denials of
contentions are warranted. Fed. R. Civ. P. 11(b)
[177]. Hence, counsel must make a reasonable

inquiry into the facts and law in preparing the
answer.

B.   ADMITTING OR DENYING THE
ALLEGATIONS IN THE COMPLAINT

Under federal rules, a defendant must "fairly
respond to the substance of the allegation," Rule
8(b)(2) [366], which usually means responding to
each individual allegation specifically.   Only if a
defendant intends to deny *every* allegation,
including allegations regarding jurisdiction and the
identity of the parties, may he file what is called a
general denial. Fed. R. Civ. P. 8(b)(3) [367]; *see also*,
e.g., Fla. R. Civ. P. 1.110(c) [165]; Tenn. R. Civ. P.
8.02 [508]. Some states, however, allow a defendant
to file a general denial as long as the complaint is
not verified—that is, signed under oath by the
plaintiff. *See* Cal. Code Civ. P. 431.30(d) [142]; Tex.
R. Civ. P. 92 [505].

Defendants' options in responding to an allegation
are to (1) admit it, (2) deny it, (3) admit it in part
and deny it in part, or (4) state the defendant is
without sufficient information or belief as to the
truth of the allegation (which has the effect of a
denial). Fed. R. Civ. P. 8(b)(5) [369]. "Responding to
the substance of an allegation" requires "a party
that intends in good faith to deny only part of an
allegation must admit the part that is true and deny
the rest." Fed. R. Civ. P. 8(b)(4) [368].   Counsel
should keep in mind, however, that any allegation,
except an allegation regarding the amount of

damages, that is not denied will be deemed admitted. Fed. R. Civ. P. 8(b)(6) [370].

C. AFFIRMATIVE DEFENSES

Defendants must also assert in the answer any affirmative defenses they have against the plaintiff's claims or risk waiving those defenses. Rule 8(c)(1) [371] provides: "In responding to a pleading, a party must affirmatively state *any avoidance or affirmative defense*, including: accord and satisfaction; arbitration and award; assumption of risk; contributory negligence; duress; estoppel; failure of consideration; fraud; illegality; injury by fellow servant; laches; license; payment; release; res judicata; statute of frauds; statute of limitations; and waiver" (emphasis added).

This list of defenses is not exclusive, however. Although Rule 8 [360] does not further define "any avoidance or affirmative defense," generally "an affirmative defense is an 'assertion of facts and arguments that, if true, will defeat the plaintiff's . . . claim, even if all the allegations in the complaint are true.'" *Starnes Family Office, LLC v. McCullar*, 765 F. Supp. 2d 1036, 1048 (W.D. Tenn. 2011) [120] (quoting Black's Law Dictionary (9th ed. 2009) and holding the assertion that the plaintiff was incompetent under state law was not an affirmative defense, because even if the plaintiff were adjudged an incompetent, the defendant would not be relieved of liability). Also, Rule 12(h) [191] provides that defenses based on Rule 12(b)(2) [182] lack of personal jurisdiction, (3) [184] improper venue, (4)

[185] insufficient process, and (5) [186] insufficient service of process, will be waived unless raised by motion or in the answer. Thus, even if the defendant were to specifically deny an allegation in the complaint that venue was proper, he would still have to plead improper venue under Rule 12(b)(3) [184] as an affirmative defense.

Attorneys preparing an answer should err on the side of inclusion when deciding whether a position, argument, or contention should be pled as an affirmative defense. The starting point would be the list of 18 affirmative defenses set out in Rule 8(c)(1) [371]. If after a reasonable investigation, an attorney believes there are grounds for any of these, or analogous defenses, she should assert those defenses in separate paragraphs in the answer. Also, any defenses based on Rule 12(b)(2)–(5) [183] should be pled as affirmative defenses. In fact, many attorneys affirmatively plead all defenses they have under Rule 12(b) [180], especially Rule 12(b)(6) [187], because they are specifically authorized to be pled in the answer. *See* Fed. R. Civ. P. 12(h) [191]. Counsel should also include any defenses they have that courts have already categorized as affirmative defenses. For example, the failure to mitigate damages is a well-recognized affirmative defense that is not listed in Rule 8(c)(1) [371]. *See Sayre v. Musicland Group, Inc., a Subsidiary of American Can Co.*, 850 F.2d 350, 353–54 (8th Cir. 1988) [123]. Then, any other reason the defendant has for why the plaintiff should not prevail that goes beyond simply denying an allegation should be asserted as an affirmative defense. Just as the complaint may contain inconsistent claims, the answer may contain inconsistent defenses. Fed. R. Civ. P. 8(d) [372]. So, for example, in response to a breach of contract action, the defendant may assert both that the plaintiff breached the contract and that there was no valid offer—meaning no contract was formed. Finally, to avoid any confusion, affirmative defenses should be set out in separate paragraphs under the heading "Affirmative Defenses."

D. COUNTERCLAIMS AND CROSSCLAIMS

1. Generally

Before drafting the answer, the attorney should assess whether the defendant has any claims against other parties in the action. Generally, claims a defendant has against the plaintiff are known as *counterclaims*, while claims against other defendants are known as *crossclaims*. The answer *must* contain any "compulsory counterclaims" the defendant has against the plaintiff, and *may* contain any other counterclaim and crossclaims. Fed. R. Civ. P. 13(a), (b) & (g) [193].

2. Compulsory counterclaims

If the answer does not contain a claim against the defendant that is a compulsory counterclaim, that claim is thereafter barred. A compulsory counterclaim is an existing claim that "(A) arises out of the transaction or occurrence that is the subject matter of the opposing party's claim; and (B) does not require adding another party over whom the court cannot acquire jurisdiction." Fed. R. Civ. P. 13(a), (b) & (g) [193]. The reason for making these types of claims compulsory is to avoid duplicative future litigation involving the same facts. Thus, these factors are considered in determining if a counterclaim is compulsory: "(1) Are the issues of fact and law raised in the claim and counterclaim largely the same? (2) Would res judicata bar a subsequent suit on the party's counterclaim, absent the compulsory counterclaim rule? (3) Will substantially the same evidence support or refute the claim as well as the counterclaim? and (4) Is there any logical relationship between the claim and counterclaim?" *Painter v. Harvey*, 863 F.2d 329, 331 (4th Cir. 1988) [124].[10]

However, even if a counterclaim would be considered compulsory, a defendant is not required to assert it in the answer if (1) the counterclaim was already part of another action when the complaint was filed, or (2) if the plaintiff brought an action by attachment or other process not resulting in personal jurisdiction but only in rem or quasi in rem

---

[10] The answer to all four questions need not be yes. *Painter v. Harvey*, 863 F.2d at 331   These questions are factors or indicators, rather than elements or requirements. Their "underlying thread" is "evidentiary similarity." *Id.* [124] Thus, in *Painter v. Harvey* the court held that in a civil rights action against a police officer alleging excessive force, the officer's claims against the plaintiff for libel and slander were compulsory counterclaims. On the other hand, in *Williams v. Long*, 558 F. Supp. 2d 601, 603–04 (D. Md. 2008) [112], the court held that in an action for failure to pay minimum wage and overtime, the defendant's counterclaim for breach of contract based on falsification of work experience was not compulsory.

jurisdiction.[11] Fed. R. Civ. P. 13(a)(2) [195]; *Baker v. Gold Seal Liquors, Inc.*, 417 U.S. 467, 469 n. 1 (1974) [88] .

3. Permissive Counterclaims

A defendant may also assert permissive counterclaims in the answer. A permissive counterclaim is any claim the defendant has against the plaintiff that is not compulsory. Fed. R. Civ. P. 13(b) [196]. A permissive counterclaim, just like any other claim, however, is subject to dismissal for lack of subject matter or personal jurisdiction, failure to state a claim for which relief can be granted, and the like. *See, e.g.*, Fed. R. Civ. P. 12(b) [180]; *United States for Use and Benefit of*

---

[11] There are three types of jurisdiction: in personam, in rem, and quasi in rem jurisdiction. In personam jurisdiction refers to "[a] court's power to bring a person into its adjudicative process; jurisdiction over a defendant's personal rights, rather than merely over property interests." BLACK'S LAW DICTIONARY 930 (9th ed. 2009). For example, a court exercises its in personam jurisdiction over an individual to whom it grants a divorce and restores that person to the status of a single individual. In rem jurisdiction refers to "[a] court's power to adjudicate the rights to a given piece of property, including the power to seize and hold it." BLACK'S LAW DICTIONARY 929 (9th ed. 2009). For example, the court exercises its in rem jurisdiction when a case involves a particular piece of property, such as when the court oversees the administration of a decedent's estate. Quasi in rem jurisdiction is "[j]urisdiction over a person but based on that person's interest in property located within the court's territory." BLACK'S LAW DICTIONARY 930 (9th ed. 2009). For example, the court's power to preside over a judicial foreclosure over a mortgage is an exercise of the court's quasi in rem jurisdiction; the court is exercising its jurisdiction over a person's rights in property located within its jurisdiction.

Kashulines v. Thermo Contracting Corp., 437 F. Supp. 195, 199 (D. N.J. 1976) [90].

4. Crossclaims

A defendant, in the answer, may also assert crossclaims against other defendants in the litigation.   A crossclaim is a claim against a co-defendant that "arises out of the transaction or occurrence that is the subject matter of the original action or of a counterclaim, or . . . relates to any property that is the subject matter of the original action." Fed. R. Civ. P. 13(g) [197]. In other words, a crossclaim would qualify as a compulsory counterclaim if it were asserted against the plaintiff or it relates to property at issue in complaint.

IV. ANSWER FILED BY DEFENDANTS IN *NEELY V. FOX*

On July 7, 2005, counsel representing both Fox of Oak Ridge, Inc. and Benjamin H. Curd filed an answer [467] to the complaint [407] in the United States District Court for the Eastern District of Tennessee, Northern Division. Please review that answer [467] and respond to the following questions.

1. Which allegations in the complaint are admitted? Which paragraphs of the answer contain these admissions?

2. Which allegations in the complaint are denied? Which paragraphs of the answer contain these denials?

3. Which allegations of the complaint are admitted in part and denied in part? Which paragraphs of the answer contain the partial admission and denials?

4. Are there any allegations in the complaint to which the defendants state they have insufficient information to admit or deny? If so, which allegations, and which paragraph of the answer contains this response?

5. Read paragraph 9 of the answer. Why do you think the defendant's counsel included this response?

6. Does the answer contain any affirmative defenses? If yes, what defenses are alleged?

7. Can you think of any other affirmative defenses that the defendant might have had?

8. Does the answer contain any counterclaims? If yes, what claims are alleged?

9. Can you think of any counterclaims the defendants might have had against the plaintiff?

CHAPTER 4

PROCEEDING BEFORE A
MAGISTRATE JUDGE

I.   OVERVIEW

Supreme Court justices and judges of the United States Courts of Appeal and District Court are nominated by the President and confirmed by the Senate pursuant to Article III, section 1 of the Constitution. Commonly referred to as "Article III judges," they have lifetime tenure, subject to the condition of good behavior and protection from reductions in salary. U.S. Const., art III, § 1 [636]. Magistrate judges are non-Article III federal judges who serve in district courts for eight year terms; they do not have the Constitutional protections of lifetime tenure or protection from reduction in salary. They are appointed by the Article III judges of a district court based on the recommendation of a merit selection panel.   28 U.S.C. § 631(b)(5) [61]. Magistrate judges are supervised by district judges whom they help to manage the district courts' ever increasing caseloads. *Roell v. Withrow*, 538 U.S. 580, 588 (2003) [109].   A magistrate judge's involvement in a case originates in two ways, either by (1) referral of particular matters to the magistrate by a district judge, 28 U.S.C. § 636(b)(1), or (2) [67] consent of the parties to the jurisdiction of a magistrate judge, 28 U.S.C. § 636(c)(1) [69].

II. REFERRALS BY DISTRICT JUDGES

A district judge may designate a magistrate judge to hear and determine non-dispositive pre-trial matters—that is, "any pretrial matter pending before the court, except a motion for injunctive relief, for judgment on the pleadings, for summary judgment, to dismiss or quash an indictment or information made by the defendant, to suppress evidence in a criminal case, to dismiss or to permit maintenance of a class action, to dismiss for failure to state a claim upon which relief can be granted, and to involuntarily dismiss an action." 28 U.S.C. § 636(b)(1)(A) [65]. Matters involving pre-trial discovery disputes are often referred to magistrate judges. "Discovery" refers to the process and stage of the case where the parties disclose and gather factual information regarding the case. There are a variety of rules governing what type of information is accessible to the other side and what type may be withheld. A magistrate judge might, for example, determine whether a certain document was privileged from disclosure because it was a confidential communication between an attorney and her client. The district judge may reconsider any matter decided under § 636(b)(1)(A) [65] if a party has shown the decision of the magistrate judge "is clearly erroneous or contrary to law."

In addition, a district judge may designate a magistrate judge to conduct hearings on dispositive pretrial matters, i.e., the matters excepted in § 636(b)(1)(A) [65], and submit to the district judge proposed findings of fact and recommendations for disposition of the matter. The district judge "may accept, reject, or modify, in whole or in part, the findings or recommendations made by the magistrate judge. The judge may also receive further evidence or recommit the matter to the magistrate judge with instructions." 28 U.S.C. § 636(b)(1)(B) [66]. The district judge's review of the findings and recommendations is de novo, in the capacity of a trial court, with no presumption or deference to the magistrate's report. This is different from an appellate review, which is generally de novo with regard to questions of law (because the appellate court is in the same position as a trial court) and deferential with regard to questions of fact (since the trial court heard the testimony and saw the witnesses and the exhibits and the appellate court did not).

III. CONSENT OF THE PARTIES TO THE JURISDICTION OF A MAGISTRATE JUDGE

If a magistrate judge has been specifically designated to exercise jurisdiction, the parties may consent to his or her jurisdiction over the entire case—meaning the magistrate judge "may conduct any or all proceedings [including trial] in a jury or nonjury civil matter and order the entry of judgment in the case." Also, any judgment or final order the magistrate judge enters is directly appealable to the United States Court of Appeals in that circuit. 28 U.S.C. § 636(c)(1) &(3) [70]; Fed. R. Civ. P. 73(a) & (c) [355]. Consenting to the jurisdiction of a magistrate judge often results in an earlier trial date and a swifter process overall.

Magistrate judges, unlike district court judges, may try only misdemeanor criminal cases, not felonies which are generally more complicated and time consuming and which take priority over civil cases on the court's docket. 28 U.S.C. § 636(a)(3) [62]. Thus, a magistrate judge may have more room on his or her docket for civil cases. In addition, consenting to the jurisdiction of a magistrate judge avoids the sometimes time consuming process of review by the district court of the magistrate's report and recommendations that is required when a matter is referred to the magistrate judge by a district court without the parties' consent. *See* 28 U.S.C. § 636(b)(1) [64].

If a magistrate judge has been specifically designated to exercise jurisdiction, the clerk of court must notify the parties that:

(1) a magistrate judge is available to hear any or all proceedings if all parties consent;

(2) to signify their consent, they must file a statement with the court consenting to the referral; and

(3) they may withhold their consent without adverse consequences.

Fed. R. Civ. P. 73(b)(1) & (2) [356]. A district or magistrate judge may be informed of the parties' responses only if all parties have consented to the referral. Fed. R. Civ. P. 73(b)(1) [356]. This prevents the bias that could result from knowing

which parties resisted assignment of the matter to
the magistrate.

On July 19, 2005, the clerk's office sent the
parties in *Neely v. Fox* a Notice of Availability of a
Magistrate Judge to Exercise Jurisdiction. All
parties consented to the exercise of jurisdiction by a
magistrate judge. On August 19, 2005, District
Judge Thomas W. Phillips referred [474] the matter
to Magistrate Judge H. Bruce Guyton for all
proceedings and entry of judgment.

QUESTIONS

Review the Notice of Availability of Magistrate Judge
[474] and Rule 73(b)(1) & (2) [356].

1. Does the notice comply with the requirements of
    Rule 73?

2. Does the notice contain additional information
    not required by Rule 73? If yes, what additional
    information is included?

3. Why do you think the parties in *Neely v. Fox*
    consented to the jurisdiction of a magistrate
    judge?

CHAPTER 5
CASE MANAGEMENT AND SCHEDULING

I. OVERVIEW

The Federal Rules of Civil Procedure "should be construed and administered to secure the just, speedy, and inexpensive determination of every action and proceeding." FED. R. CIV. P. 1 [171]. The term "administered" was added to Rule 1 in 1993 to make it explicit that courts "have an affirmative duty to ensure that civil litigation is resolved not only fairly, but also without undue cost or delay. As officers of the court, attorneys share this responsibility with the judge to whom the case is assigned." FED. R. CIV. P. 1 [170], advisory committee's note (1993). Case management is the process by which judges, with the cooperation of counsel, help accomplish the just, speedy, and inexpensive resolution of civil actions. William W. Schwarzer and Alan Hirsch, *The Elements of Case Management: A Pocket Guide for Judges*, p.1 (2d ed. Federal Judicial Center 2006) [161].

Case management and scheduling in federal district courts is governed primarily by Rule 16 [200], which authorizes pre-trial conferences to control and manage cases and prescribes the contents of the scheduling order that controls the timing of events in the case. District courts also promulgate their own local rules for fair and efficient case management. In addition, individual judges often have specific rules, procedures, or preferences for case management. Click here for Magistrate Judge Guyton's list of judicial preferences [480].

II. RULE 16 CONFERENCES

One of the most important tools in case management is the Rule 16 [200] conference or "scheduling conference." This conference is usually the first time a judge has contact with the attorneys. It is the judge's first opportunity to gauge what the case is about and set the tone for its fair and efficient administration. It is often stated that 20% of the cases consume 80% of the court resources. Some cases are genuinely complicated—legally, factually, or both. In other cases, however, the lawyers create much of the work—disputing points that should be stipulated to, filing needless motions, engaging in protracted discovery battles, and the like.

The purposes of a Rule 16 [200] conference are "(1) expediting disposition of the action; (2) establishing early and continuing control so that the case will not be protracted because of lack of management; (3) discouraging wasteful pretrial activities; (4) improving the quality of the trial through more thorough preparation; and (5) facilitating settlement." FED. R. CIV. P. 16(a) [201]. At a Rule 16 conference, the judge, with the help of the lawyers will narrow or discern the central issues in the case; decide what, if any, motions would be useful; establish an efficient discovery program;

explore the possibility of settlement, and set dates
for future proceedings. Thus, at the conference, at
least one lawyer on each side must be authorized to
make stipulations and admissions regarding the
case.

Ideally, Rule 16 [200] conferences are scheduled
as early as possible—before the attorneys become
too entrenched in their positions; or, on the flip side,
before they begin to procrastinate and "let things
slide." Also, the judge is required to issue the
scheduling order that follows the conference "as
soon as practicable, but in any event within the
earlier of 120 days after any defendant has been
served with the complaint or 90 days after any
defendant has appeared." FED. R. CIV. P. 16(b)(2)
[203].[12] The conference must be scheduled early
enough to allow the court enough time to meet this
time limit.

Rule 16(c)(2) [208] lists a variety of matters that
"the court may consider and take appropriate action
on" in the conference. Topping the list is
"formulating and simplifying the issues, and
eliminating frivolous claims or defenses." This
makes sense because establishing the actual pivotal
issues in the case will often control how other
matters such as motions, discovery, settlement
discussions, and scheduling are handled. Also,
although subject matter jurisdiction is not listed as

---

[12] The individual districts may exempt certain categories of
cases from the scheduling order requirement. FED. R. CIV. P.
16(b)(1) [202].

an agenda item in Rule 16(c)(2) [208], many judges will specifically address this issue in the Rule 16 conference. Lack of subject matter jurisdiction is a defect that is never waived—meaning it can be raised very late in the proceedings, including during the appeal process. Thus in the initial stages it is a good idea to expressly determine whether subject matter jurisdiction is present to avoid wasting time and resources in a case where any judgment would be void. Often the notice setting the Rule 16 conference will inform counsel of the matters to be addressed and what should be done to prepare for the conference. The Notice of Scheduling Conference [471] in *Neely v. Fox* asked counsel to review the form of the standard scheduling order available on the court's website.[13]

Shortly after the Rule 16 [200] conference, the court will usually file what is called a "minute entry"—a very short order on the docket sheet that contains the key decisions and dates set during the conference. A more detailed scheduling order will follow the minute entry. Here [473] is the minute entry regarding the Rule 16 scheduling conference in *Neely v. Fox*.[14]

III. SCHEDULING ORDERS

The scheduling order is another important case management tool. It assures that the court will have early involvement and control over the case

---

[13] The notice was issued by District Judge Thomas Philips before the action was referred to Magistrate Judge Bruce Guyton.

[14] "FPTC" stands for Final Pretrial Conference.

and helps to prevent lawyer-procrastination by setting specific deadlines for future events in the proceedings. At a minimum, the order must set deadlines or time limits for the parties to "join other parties, amend the pleadings, complete discovery, and file motions." FED. R. CIV. P. 16(b)(3)(A) [204]. The scheduling order may also set the trial date and the date of the final pretrial conference, modify the timing of required discovery disclosures and the extent of discovery, and "include other appropriate matters." FED. R. CIV. P. 16(b)(3)(B) [205]. Once a scheduling order has been issued, it "may be modified only for good cause and with the judge's consent." In other words, the lawyers may not agree among themselves to extend the deadlines or time limits set out in the scheduling order. FED. R. CIV. P. 16(b)(4) [206].

Many districts have promulgated local rules that set out further requirements for what must be contained in a scheduling order, and some have standard form scheduling orders. *See* Nancy Weeks, *District Court Implementation of Amended Civil Rule 16: A Report on New Local Rules* (Federal Judicial Center 1984) [387]. In other districts, including the Eastern District of Tennessee, where *Neely v. Fox* was filed, the individual judges and magistrate judges have standing form scheduling orders that are accessible on the court's website. Here [383] is the standard form scheduling order for Magistrate Judge Guyton, and here [408] is the scheduling order he entered in *Neely v. Fox*.

QUESTIONS

1. When did the Rule 16 Scheduling Conference take place in *Neely v. Fox*?

2. What documents in the court file show when the conference occurred?

3. Did the conference take place within the time limits prescribed in Rule 16(b)(1) [202]?

4. Review the standard form scheduling order for Magistrate Judge Guyton and the scheduling order [408] he entered in *Neely v. Fox*. Are there any subjects or items in the *Neely v. Fox* scheduling order that are not included in the standard form scheduling order? If yes, what are they?

5. Does the *Neely v. Fox* scheduling order include the required contents specified in Rule 16(b)(3)(A) [204]?

6. What paragraphs of the scheduling order contain the contents required in Rule 16(b)(3)(A) [204]?

7. What other subjects does the scheduling order address and in which paragraphs?

8. Based on your review of the scheduling order, do you think the scheduling conference in *Neely v. Fox* fulfilled the purposes of Rule 16(a) [201]?

CHAPTER 6
DISCOVERY

I. OVERVIEW

"Discovery" is the process by which the parties learn facts that pertain to the lawsuit from the other or third parties. In federal civil actions, the first phase of discovery consists of mandatory disclosures by the parties of basic information regarding their claims, defenses, damages, and insurance. Other methods of discovery include depositions, interrogatories, requests for production of documents, subpoenas duces tecum, physical and mental examinations, and requests for admissions. Discovery is governed by rules of civil procedure and managed by the parties, as well as by the court. Disclosures and discovery are exchanged by the parties and are generally not filed with the court unless they are related to a motion or other court proceeding.

The scope of discovery in federal civil cases is defined in Rule 26 of the Federal Rules of Civil Procedure. In general, "parties may obtain discovery regarding any nonprivileged matter that is relevant to any party's claim or defense—including the existence, description, nature, custody, condition, and location of any documents or other tangible things and the identity and location of persons who know of any discoverable matter." FED. R. CIV. P. 26(b)(1) [231]. Also, "for good cause, the court may order discovery of any matter relevant to the subject matter involved in the action." *Id.* [231] Discoverable information need not be admissible at trial, as long as it "appears reasonably calculated to lead to the discovery of admissible evidence." FED. R. CIV. P. 26(b)(1) [231]. However, even if information sought is relevant, it is generally not discoverable if it is privileged, e.g., if it contains confidential attorney-client communications or constitutes attorney "work product"—that is, materials prepared by counsel in anticipation of litigation. FED. R. CIV. P. 26(b)(1) & (3) [232]. Also, a court may limit discovery that would otherwise be allowed if it is unreasonably cumulative, burdensome, or expensive to the responding party. *See* FED. R. CIV. P. 26(b)(2) [233].

In most federal civil actions, the attorneys are responsible for arranging an initial discovery conference to take place at least 21 days before the Rule 16 scheduling conference is held or the scheduling order is due. FED. R. CIV. P. 26(f)(1) [242]. In the discovery conference counsel "must consider the nature and basis of their claims and defenses and the possibilities for settl[ement]; make or arrange for the disclosures required by Rule 26(a)(1) [222]; discuss any issues about preserving discoverable information; and develop a proposed discovery plan." FED. R. CIV. P. 26(f)(2) [243]. The proposed discovery plan must address: the timing and sequence of the initial disclosures and discovery, including when discovery should be concluded; the subjects on which discovery may be needed and whether discovery should be limited or focused on particular issues; any issues regarding the disclosure or discovery of electronic information; and any issues regarding claims of privilege. FED. R. CIV. P. 26(f)(3) [244]. Note, however, that a court may waive the requirements that the parties hold an initial discovery conference and submit a proposed discovery plan. FED. R. CIV. P. 26(f)(1) [242].

There is a tension in the literature discussing discovery practice of which you should be aware, even though we will not go into it in detail in this book. If one reads the discovery rules and many of the cases and secondary sources, one could form the impression that the discovery process is largely consensual, undertaken in good faith, and efficient. While it is certainly possible—and *Neely v. Fox* is a great example of discovery and pre-trial practice done right—it is also possible for counsel to engage in aggressive discovery practices using broad objections, unwarranted interpretations of requests, overbroad motions for protective orders, and motions to compel. Much of the most flagrant, bad, and often unprofessional conduct between counsel takes place out of court, in discovery, particularly in depositions. So, there is a tension between what can look on its face like a simple, professional, efficient system for learning about the facts, claims, and defenses in a lawsuit and the decidedly uncivil way in which the process can play out as litigious counsel engage in direct confrontation outside of the sight of the judge.

II. DISCOVERY DEVICES

A.   REQUIRED DISCLOSURES—RULE 26(a)

Rule 26(a) requires the parties to disclose certain information without waiting for a formal discovery request. The information is the kind usually necessary to prepare for trial or to evaluate the advantages of settlement. Early on in the case, the parties must exchange information regarding potential witnesses and documents that may be used to support their claims or defenses, as well as information regarding damages and potential insurance. FED. R. CIV. P. 26(a)(1) [222]. These Rule 26(a)(1)(A) disclosures are known as "initial disclosures" and their main purpose is to speed up the exchange of basic information about the case. *See* FED. R. CIV. P. 26, advisory committee's note (1993) [228].

Later in the discovery process the parties must disclose the identity of any expert witness they expect to use at trial and provide a detailed report of the testimony he or she will offer. FED. R. CIV. P. 26(a)(2) [224]. Finally, close to the trial date the parties must identify the witnesses, documents, and other evidence they intend to use at trial. FED. R. CIV. P. 26(a)(3) [225]. These are known as "pre-trial disclosures."

B.   DEPOSITIONS—RULE 30

A deposition is testimony of a witness taken out of court and under oath. In a deposition, the attorneys for each party ask the witness (called the "deponent") questions, and the questions' answers are recorded usually by a stenographer or video or both. FED. R. CIV. P. 30(a) [249]. Depositions are one of the most useful and widely used discovery tools. They enable attorneys to find out a great deal of factual information from parties and other key witnesses, especially due to their "conversational" nature, which allows the deposing attorney to ask follow up questions in response to a deponent's responses, something that cannot as easily and effectively be done with paper discovery, like interrogatories (described below). They also allow both sides to assess the demeanor and potential effectiveness of potential witnesses at trial and evaluate the potential for settlement. Depositions are also used to generate testimony to be used at trial, as was the case in *Neely v. Fox*—where video depositions of the plaintiff's physicians were played for the jury.

A party intending to depose a witness must give written notice to the other parties stating the time and place of the deposition, the identity of the deponent, and the method of recording the testimony. FED. R. CIV. P. 30(b)(1) & (3) [250]. If the deponent is a party, the service of the notice of deposition is enough to compel attendance. Non-parties, however, must also be served with a subpoena [491] prepared by counsel and issued by the court in order to compel their attendance. FED. R. CIV. P. 45(a) [294]. Here is an example of a notice of deposition and subpoena of a non-party deponent [476].

Under a Rule 30(b)(6) [252] a party may take the deposition of an entity such as a corporation. The notice of deposition (if the entity is a party) or subpoena (if the entity is a non-party) "must describe with reasonable particularity the matters for examination." The entity must then designate "one or more officers, directors, or managing agents" to testify on its behalf. "The persons designated must testify about information known or reasonably available to the organization." FED. R. CIV. P. 30(b)(6) [252].

A party may also require the deponent to produce documents and other materials at the deposition— using a subpoena duces tecum for non parties and a request for production of documents under Rule 34 [263] for parties. FED. R. CIV. P. 30(b)(2) [251].

Generally, the attorney who noticed the deposition will ask the deponent the majority of questions, seeking to find out facts about the case, as well as to attempt to expose any weaknesses on the other side. Before the deponent answers any question, his or her attorney, as well as the attorneys for the other parties, may object for the record on evidentiary grounds to the form of the question, etc. The deponent must answer the question, however, unless her attorney instructs her not to—usually to preserve a privilege. FED. R. CIV. P. 30(c)(2) [254]. After the direct examination, the attorney representing the deponent and attorneys representing other parties may ask the deponent questions. FED. R. CIV. P. 30(c)(1) [253]. The deponent is afforded a chance to review the transcript or other recording and make any corrections or changes. FED. R. CIV. P. 30(e) [255]. The final transcript is not filed with the court unless and until it is to be used to support a motion or for evidentiary purposes at trial.

C.   INTERROGATORIES—RULE 33

Interrogatories are written questions from one party to another party in the lawsuit. In federal civil actions, they are governed by FED. R. CIV. P. 33 [258]. Interrogatories are useful to expand or follow-up on the mandatory disclosures required in Rule 26(a) [221]. For example Rule 26(a)(1)(A)(i) [223] requires parties to identify persons with information they may use to support their claims or defenses. A party could use interrogatories to ask for the identity of *any* person with *any* information regarding the other party's claims and defenses (regardless of whether the party intends to use that information), as well as a description of the type of information possessed by each person identified in the response.

Also under Rule 33(a)(2) [260], an interrogatory may ask for or about an opinion, contention, or the application of law to facts. Thus a party may ask the other party to describe the factual or legal basis for its claims or defenses, e.g., "Please describe the facts supporting your contention that the defendant was negligent" or "On what legal theory do you base your claim for rescission? What facts support this theory?"

Generally, a party may serve up to 25 interrogatories on any other party, although this number may be increased by stipulation of the parties or court order. FED. R. CIV. P. 33(a)(1) [259]. After being served with interrogatories, a party has 30 days to respond to them by fully answering under oath, or objecting to, each interrogatory. FED. R. CIV. P. 33(b)(2) & (3) [261]. The grounds for objecting to an interrogatory must be stated specifically. FED. R. CIV. P. 33(b)(4) [262]. Common objections are the interrogatory (1) is irreleviant; (2) is unduly burdensome; or (3) inquires into matters that are privileged, e.g., attorney-client communications.

D.   REQUESTS FOR PRODUCTION OF DOCUMENTS—RULE 34 AND SUBPOENAS DUCES TECUM—RULE 45

A party may also inspect non-priviliged documents and other materials that are relevant to the claims and defenses in the lawsuit. If the materials are in the possession, custody, or control of another party to the suit, this is accomplished by serving the party with a request for production of documents or other tangible things under FED. R. CIV. P. 34 [263]. If the materials are in the possession, custody, or control of a third party, a subpoena duces tecum must be obtained from the clerk of court and served on the third party. FED. R. CIV. P. 34(c) [271] and 45(a)–(c) [297].

Rules 34 and 45 cover a wide variety of materials— specifically:

(A) any designated documents or electronically stored information—including writings, drawings, graphs, charts, photographs, sound recordings, images, and other data or data compilations—stored in any medium from which information can be obtained either directly or, if necessary, after translation by the responding party into a reasonably usable form; or

(B) any designated tangible things.

FED. R. CIV. P. 34(a)(1)(A) & (B) [264]; *see also* FED. R. CIV. P. 45(a)(1)(A)(iii) [296].

A request for production "(A) must describe with reasonable particularity each item or category of items to be inspected; (B) must specify a reasonable time, place, and manner for the inspection and for performing the related acts; and (C) may specify the form or forms in which electronically stored information is to be produced." FED. R. CIV. P. 34(b)(1) [265]; *see also* FED. R. CIV. P. 45(a)(1) [295] (form and contents of subpoenas).

The party receiving the request has 30 days to respond. FED. R. CIV. P. 34(b)(2)(A) [266]. For each item or category of items requested, the responding party must either state that the inspection will be permitted or the items produced as requested or object to the request stating the reasons for the objection. FED. R. CIV. P. 34(b)(2)(B) [267]. Also, an objection to part of a request must specify which part and permit inspection of the rest. FED. R. CIV. P. 34(b)(2)(C) [268]. Typical objections are (1) the request is vague or overbroad; (2) the request is unduly burdensome or expensive; (3) the items requested are not relevant to the claims or defenses in action; or (4) the items requested are privileged. Non-parties served with a subpoena duces tecum may also object to the inspection or production of the items specified, although the objections "must be served before the earlier of the time specified for compliance or 14 days after the subpoena is served." FED. R. CIV. P. 45(c)(2)(B) [298].

Documents and electronically stored information must be produced in a coherent fashion. A party or person responding to a request for documents or subpoena duces tecum "must produce documents as they are kept in the usual course of business or must organize and label them to correspond to the categories in the request." FED. R. CIV. P. 34(b)(2)(E)(i) [269]; 45(d)(1)(A) [299]. The point is to prevent parties from dumping a deliberately disorganized mass of documents upon their opponents, driving up the legal fees associated with their review. If the request or subpoena "does not specify a form for producing electronically stored information, a party must produce it in a form or forms in which it is ordinarily maintained or in a reasonably usable form or forms." FED. R. CIV. P. 34(b)(2)(E)(ii) [270]; 45(d)(1)(B) [300].

Occasionally, privileged documents are inadvertently produced, particularly in cases involving the production of a great many documents. If this occurs, both Rule 26 [220] and Rule 45 [293] provide a safety net. In the event of an inadvertent disclosure, the party or person claiming the privilege may notify the party who received the information of the claim of privilege and its basis. "After being notified, a party must promptly return, sequester, or destroy the specified information and any copies it has; must not use or disclose the information until the claim is resolved; must take reasonable steps to retrieve the information if the party disclosed it before being notified; and may promptly present the information to the court under seal for a determination of the claim. The [party or] person who produced the information must preserve the information until the claim is resolved." FED. R. CIV. P. 26(b)(5)(B) [235]; 45(d)(2)(B) [301].

E.   PHYSICAL AND MENTAL EXAMINATIONS—RULE 35

Where a party's physical or mental condition is in controversy, a court may order that party to submit to an independent physical or mental examination, i.e., one conducted by someone other than the party's own doctor. FED. R. CIV. P. 35(a)(1) [274]. The court may also order a person in a party's custody or under the party's legal control to submit such an examination. *Id.* Thus, for example, a parent suing to recover for injuries to a minor may be ordered to produce the minor for examination. FED. R. CIV. P. 35 [273], advisory committee's notes (1970).

The rule states that an examination may be issued "only on motion for good cause" and "must specify the time, place, manner, conditions, and scope of the examination, as well as the person or persons who will perform it." FED. R. CIV. P. 35(a)(2) [275]. Usually, when it is clear that a party's mental or physical condition is in controversy, e.g., in a personal injury case, the parties will stipulate to an independent examination after agreeing on its parameters.

F.   REQUESTS FOR ADMISSION—RULE 36

A party may serve any other party with requests for admission on matters relevant to the lawsuit. Requests for admission may ask parties to admit the truth of matters within the scope of discovery "relating to (A) facts, the application of law to fact, or opinions about either and (B) the genuineness of any described documents." FED. R. CIV. P. 36(a)(1)(A) & (B) [277]. Requests for admissions are useful tools for narrowing the facts and issues that are actually in dispute and authenticating documents that likely will be used as exhibits at trial. Note that "an admission under this [Rule 36] [276] is not an admission for any other purpose and cannot be used against the party in any other proceeding." FED. R. CIV. P. 36(b) [282].

Generally, a party has 30 days to respond to requests for admissions, otherwise they will be deemed admitted, although a shorter or longer time to respond may be stipulated to by the parties or ordered by the court. FED. R. CIV. P. 36(a)(3) [278]. As to each request for admission, a party may (1) admit, (2) deny, (3) admit in part and deny in part,

(4) admit in part and qualify in part, (5) explain in detail why the party cannot admit or deny the request, or (6) object, specifying the grounds. FED. R. CIV. P. 36(a)(4) & (5) [279]. Common objections are that the request is beyond the allowable scope of discovery or asks about matters that are privileged, e.g., attorney-client communications or attorney work product. A party may not object on the grounds that the request presents a genuine issue for trial, e.g., whether the defendant is negligent. FED. R. CIV. P. 36(a)(5) [280].

A requesting party may move the court to determine the sufficiency of an answer or objection. "Unless the court finds an objection justified, it must order that an answer be served. On finding that an answer does not comply with this rule, the court may order either that the matter is admitted or that an amended answer be served." FED. R. CIV. P. 36(a)(6) [281].

To avoid having to resort to the court, counsel drafting requests for admission should make sure each request is narrow, specific, and largely lacking in adjectives, adverbs, or other characterizations and interpretations; otherwise the request is likely to be objected to or denied.

III. DISCOVERY DISPUTES

Discovery disputes are often time consuming, expensive, and a drain on court resources. Hence courts, aided by procedural rules, encourage litigants to resolve disputes on their own or with the help of a case management conference rather than through formal motions and hearings. The objectives of the party propounding discovery and those of the responding party are often diametrically opposed. In propounding discovery, the objective is generally to find out as much information as possible, to cast the widest net possible. In responding to discovery and making initial disclosures under Rule 26(a) [221], the objective is usually to give up as little information as possible, particularly information that might be damaging. Several procedural rules are aimed at compelling parties and their counsel to be equitable, accurate, and rational in their approach to discovery. As noted in the overview above, although this is the way that the system should operate, that is not always the case and heated and protracted disputes that eventually require resolution by the court abound. It is safe to say that, of all the civil matters that occupy a court's docket, discovery disputes are among those that judges most dislike.

First, Rule 26(f) [241], discussed in section I, above, provides for counsel to confer early on in the case and propose a discovery plan. Also, Rule 26(g) [245], discovery's equivalent to Rule 11, requires disclosures, discovery requests, responses, and objections to be signed by at least one attorney of record or the party if unrepresented. By signing, the attorney or party certifies that: (1) disclosures are complete and accurate at the time made; and (2) discovery requests, responses, or objections are consistent with the law and the rules of civil procedure; are not made for any improper purpose such as to harass, cause delay, or add expense; and are not unduly burdensome or expensive. Parties, their attorneys, or both are subject to sanctions for violations of this rule. FED. R. CIV. P. 26(g)(3) [246].

A party seeking to prevent or limit certain discovery, whether it is a deposition, the production of documents, answering certain interrogatories, or requests for admission, etc., may file a motion for a protective order. FED. R. CIV. P. 26(c) [236]. However, "[t]he motion must include a certification that the movant has in good faith conferred or attempted to confer with other affected parties in an effort to resolve the dispute without court action." *Id.* For good cause shown, the court has many options in fashioning a protective order, from preventing or limiting discovery to prescribing the specific circumstances in which discovery may be obtained. FED. R. CIV. P. 26(c)(1)(A)–(H) [237]. The court may also order that discovery be provided or permitted. FED. R. CIV. P. 26(c)(2) [239].

A party seeking disclosures or discovery may file a motion to compel. FED. R. CIV. P. 37 [283]. The other party may have refused to provide disclosures or discovery, or the disclosures or discovery provided may have been incomplete or evasive. FED. R. CIV. P. 37(a)(3)–(4) [285]. As with a motion for a protective order, a motion to compel "must include a certification that the movant has in good faith conferred or attempted to confer with the person or party failing to make disclosure or discovery in an effort to obtain it without court action." FED. R. CIV. P. 37(a)(1) [284]. The court may order that specific disclosures or discovery be provided, or issue a protective order as authorized in Rule 26(c) [236]. FED. R. CIV. P. 37(a)(5) [286]. In addition, both attorneys' fees and a wide variety of sanctions are available under Rule 37 for failure to provide discovery, violation of orders to provide discovery, and motions to compel or oppositions to motions to compel that were not substantially justified. FED. R. CIV. P. 37(a)(5)(A)–(C) , (b)–(c) [287].

IV. DISCOVERY IN *NEELY V. FOX*

Discovery in *Neely v. Fox* proceeded smoothly and did not require resolution of any disputes by the court. The deposition of Thomas Koenig, M.D., one of the doctors who treated the plaintiff, was taken on November 30, 2005, and recorded by video and stenographer. The deposition transcript [423] was filed with the court because it was the subject of a motion in limine before trial,[15] not because Dr. Koenig's deposition was the subject of a discovery dispute. The only motion regarding discovery was a Joint Motion for Order Allowing Defendant Access to Plaintiff's Medical Records [411] which was filed on December 1, 2005, along with an agreed proposed order [409] setting out the circumstances and parameters of the defendant's access. This order [412] was signed by Magistrate Judge Guyton and filed on December 5, 2005. Since medical and employment records are subject to privileges from disclosure, obtaining an agreed order for their

---

[15] Motions in limine as discussed in Chapter 8, section III, p. 105.

disclosure was an efficient method of obtaining discovery of these records from the third parties who had possession of them, versus a subpoena duces tecum which third parties would likely challenge or question.

QUESTIONS

1. According to paragraph 4 of the scheduling order [408], the requirements under Rule 26(f) [241] that the parties hold a discovery conference and propose a discovery plan were waived by the court. Why do you think this was?

2. Review the scheduling order [408] filed in *Neely v. Fox* and answer the following questions:

    -   When were the initial disclosures due?

    -   When were the deadlines for disclosure of expert witnesses?

    -   What was the deadline for pretrial disclosures?

    -   What was the "discovery cut-off date" when discovery had to be completed?

3. What are advantages of requiring initial disclosures under Rule 26(a)(1) [222]?

4. What discovery device allows counsel to evaluate the demeanor of potential witnesses?

5. What are some particular uses for interrogatories?

6. What discovery device would a party use to gain access to the documents and things in the possession, custody, and control of *another* party?

7. What discovery device would a party use to gain access to the documents and things in the possession, custody, and control of a *third* party?

8. Review the Agreed Order to Produce Medical and Hospital Records and Employment Records [412] and answer these questions:

   • What types of records were designated—how were they described?

   • How would these documents have been useful?

   • What conditions and parameters were set out regarding the production of those records?

9. What are some chief uses for requests for admission?

10. Could a third party medical exam have been ordered for Mr. Neely under Rule 35? Why or why not?

11. What do you think are some common causes of discovery disputes?

12. Why do you think there were not any major discovery disputes in *Neely v. Fox*?

CHAPTER 7

MOTIONS FOR SUMMARY JUDGMENT OR ADJUDICATION OF ISSUES

I.   OVERVIEW

The summary judgment process is a means of disposing of claims, defenses, or the entire civil action before trial. A party moving for summary judgment of the entire action or summary adjudication of a specific issue must prove "there is no genuine dispute as to any material fact and the movant is entitled to judgment as a matter of law." FED. R. CIV. P. 56(a) [335]. Material facts are those that could affect the outcome of the case, and a genuine dispute exists if "the evidence is such that a reasonable jury could return a verdict for the nonmoving party." *Anderson v. Liberty Lobby, Inc.*, 477 U.S. 242, 248 (1986) [101]. Thus, in ruling on a motion for summary judgment, the court's "function is not [it]self to weigh the evidence and determine the truth of the matter but to determine whether there is a genuine issue for trial." *Id.* at 249 [101]. In other words, the court's role is to determine whether or not factual disputes exist, not to resolve them. If there are no material factual disputes, summary judgment or adjudication would be appropriate.

A motion for summary judgment or adjudication may be filed by any party "at any time until 30 days after the close of all discovery." Most motions for summary judgment are filed after some discovery has been conducted and evidence supporting the motion has been produced. If a party proves there is no genuine dispute as to any material fact in the lawsuit, then the entire action will be disposed of and summary judgment entered in that party's favor. Often times, however, a party will seek to resolve a particular issue regarding a claim or defense and will move for summary adjudication of that issue alone—sometimes called a "motion for partial summary judgment." In this chapter the term summary judgment may include summary adjudication of issues.

II. PROCEDURES

General motion practice in federal civil actions is governed by Federal Rule of Civil Procedure 7(b) [358], and specific procedures applicable to summary judgment motions are outlined in Rule 56 [334]. Rule 7 [354] simply requires that motions "(A) be in writing unless made during a hearing or trial; (B) state with particularity the grounds for seeking the order; and (C) state the relief sought." FED. R. CIV. P. 7(b)(1) [359]. Rule 7 [354] is generally augmented by local rules of the individual federal district courts. For example, Local Rule 7.1(a) [392] of the United States District Court for the Eastern District of Tennessee, where *Neely v. Fox* was filed, states that an "opening brief and any accompanying affidavits or other supporting material shall be served and filed with the motion," and "the answering brief and any accompanying affidavits or other material shall be served and filed" within 21 days of a dispositive motion such as one for summary judgment. These "[b]riefs shall include a concise statement of the factual and legal grounds which justify the ruling sought from the Court . . . and shall not exceed 25 pages in length unless otherwise ordered by the Court." E.D. Tenn. L.R. 7.1(b) [392].

Federal Rule of Civil Procedure 56(c)(1)(A) [337] also requires a party moving for or opposing summary judgment to provide specific citations (known as "pinpoint" or "pin" citations) to materials in the record to support any assertion that a fact is disputed or undisputed. These materials typically include "depositions, documents, electronically stored information, affidavits or declarations, stipulations (including those made for purposes of the motion only), admissions, and interrogatory answers." *Id.* [337]

Discovery materials are not automatically filed with the court at the time they are disclosed or produced. Thus, a party intending to use discovery materials must file those materials with the court— which is usually done by attaching the materials as exhibits to the moving or responsive papers or to a declaration under penalty of perjury by an authenticating witness. In addition to pin-citing to selected materials, a party may argue that the materials cited by the other side fail to establish or negate a genuine dispute of fact. FED. R. CIV. P. 56(c)(1)(B) [338]. A party may also argue that the other party cannot produce admissible evidence to support a fact that it has the burden of proving at trial. *Id.* [338]

The purpose of these procedures is to compel counsel for both parties to identify and address specific facts and supporting materials that are pertinent to the motion. Indeed, "[i]f a party fails to properly support an assertion of fact or fails to properly address another party's assertion of fact as required by Rule 56(c) [336], the court may:

(1) give an opportunity to properly support or address the fact;

(2) consider the fact undisputed for purposes of the motion;

(3) grant summary judgment if the motion and supporting materials—including the facts considered undisputed—show that the movant is entitled to it; or

(4) issue any other appropriate order."

FED. R. CIV. P. 56(e) [339]. As long as the court gives notice and a reasonable time for the parties to respond, the court may also: "(1) grant summary judgment for a nonmovant; (2) grant the motion on grounds not raised by a party; or (3) consider summary judgment on its own after identifying for the parties material facts that may not be genuinely in dispute." FED. R. CIV. P. 56(g) [341].

III. SUMMARY JUDGMENT IN PRACTICE

Although the rules and procedures surrounding summary judgment are intricate, the underlying consideration at every stage is straightforward: is there is a genuine dispute of material fact? Thus, counsel hoping to obtain summary judgment or summary adjudication of an issue should design their motion and supporting documents to be as clear and simple as possible. Arguing for 25 pages and citing to voluminous materials in an attempt to convince a judge there is no dispute of fact is likely to have the opposite effect. In other words, the more complicated the motion appears, the more matters will appear disputed, and the more likely it is that the court will deny the motion. Therefore, before undertaking the time and expense of filing a motion for summary judgment, counsel should ask themselves if they can present their position in a clear, concise manner that the court will quickly and easily grasp.

No motions for summary judgment or summary adjudication of issues were filed in *Neely v. Fox*. This is not surprising because the central issues in that case—negligence, causation, and the extent of damages—involved disputes of material fact. Also, Fox of Oak Ridge admitted the allegation in Paragraph 4 of the Complaint [407] that Benjamin Curd was acting in the scope of his employment with Fox when the accident occurred. Answer, ¶ 4 [467]. This is significant because in Tennessee and most states employers are vicariously liable for the negligence of their employees who were driving within the scope of employment. *See, e.g., Tennessee Farmers Mut. Ins. Co. v. American Mut. Liab. Ins. Co.*, 840 S.W. 2d 933, 938 (Tenn. Ct. App. 1992) [122].

If Fox of Oak Ridge had not made this admission in the answer, the plaintiff, after sufficient discovery, may well have filed a motion for summary adjudication on the issue of vicarious liability. The process might have unfolded as follows:

Discovery:

In a document request to Fox of Oak Ridge (Fox), the plaintiff requested "(1) any and all documents or electronically stored information pertaining to Benjamin Curd's employment or association with Fox and (2) any and all documents pertaining to the 1998 Chevrolet Van involved in the accident." In response, Fox produced, inter alia, (1) documents showing that at the time of the accident, Curd was a salaried employee of Fox, with the job description of "Driver/Porter," and (2) a copy of a vehicle registration showing Fox as the owner of the van involved in the accident, and (3) an auto repair invoice for the van dated July 12, 2004 (the day of the accident), signed by Benjamin Curd, and noting the van was being released to him.

The plaintiff also took Curd's deposition in which he testified under oath that on the day of the accident he was employed by Fox, and he had picked up the van at the repair shop and was on his way back to return the van to Fox when the accident occurred.

Then the plaintiff served Fox with requests for admissions. Attached to the requests were Curd's employment records for the period of the accident showing he was employed by Fox as a "Driver/Porter," the vehicle registration for the van, and the repair invoice dated and signed by Curd on the day of the accident, which had previously been produced by Fox. In separate requests, Fox was asked to admit that each document was authentic— i.e., that each was a true and correct copy of the original held by Fox. Then Fox was asked to admit:

1. On July 12, 2004, a vehicle accident occurred involving Plaintiff Thomas Neely and Defendant Benjamin Curd.

2. On July 12, 2004, Benjamin Curd was an employee of Fox of Oak Ridge, Inc.

3. Fox's job description for Benjamin Curd at that time was "Driver/Porter."

4. Benjamin Curd was driving a 1998 Chevrolet Van when the accident occurred.

5. On July 12, 2004, when the accident occurred, Fox was the registered owner of the 1998 Chevrolet Van involved in the accident at issue.

6. On July 12, 2004, Curd picked up the 1998 Chevrolet Van involved in the accident from a repair shop to return it to Fox.

In response, Fox admitted each of these requests and that the documents attached to the requests for admission were authentic.

Motion for Summary Adjudication

After reviewing this discovery, counsel for the plaintiff decided they had strong, simple grounds for a motion for summary adjudication on the issue of Fox of Oak Ridge's vicarious liability. Before starting to draft the motion and supporting brief, however, counsel drafted a proposed order granting the relief that would be sought in the motion. Drafting the order first helps counsel focus on what the motion and its supporting documents need to achieve. Here is an example [153] of what the proposed order would look like. Next, counsel gathered Fox's responses to the requests for admissions and the portion of Curd's deposition testimony that would form the evidentiary support for the motion as required in Rule 56(c)(1)(A) [337] and organized these documents into exhibits. These documents were then attached as exhibits to a declaration [148] by a paralegal[16] that each document was a true and correct copy of the original document. Finally, counsel drafted the motion for summary adjudication and brief [147] in support of the motion. In the supporting brief, the pertinent facts were laid out and matched to the pertinent law, which showed that that Neely was entitled to

---

[16] Best practice is for an attorney not to become a material witness and, thus, having someone other than counsel execute the authenticating declaration is desirable. MODEL RULES OF PROF'L CONDUCT R. 3.7.

summary adjudication that Fox was vicariously liable for any negligence on the part of its employee Curd.

Although a motion for summary adjudication was not filed in *Neely v. Fox* because the issue of Fox's vicarious liability was admitted in the Answer [467], the sample motion described above quite possibly would have been granted because it would have been simple, straightforward, and specific.

QUESTIONS

1. Why does Rule 56(c)(1)(A) [337] require counsel to provide pin-point citations to materials in the record when asserting a fact is disputed or undisputed?

2. What happens if a party fails to properly support an assertion of fact or fails to address an assertion of fact made by the other side?

3. What is the court's role in ruling on a motion for summary judgment or summary adjudication of an issue?

4. Does a court considering a motion for summary judgment or summary adjudication of an issue decide disputes of fact?

Review the sample Brief [147] in Support of the Plaintiff's Motion for Summary Adjudication on the Issue of Vicarious Liability and answer the following questions:

5. What is the purpose of the preliminary statement?

6. Review the Facts Section of the Brief. Are pin-point citations provided for each assertion of fact? How?

7. Review the Discussion Section of the argument,
    consisting of 2 paragraphs. What is discussed in
    the first paragraph? What is discussed in the
    second paragraph?

CHAPTER 8

FINAL PRE-TRIAL PROCEDURE AND PROCEEDINGS

I. OVERVIEW

The final month before trial is a busy time for counsel in a civil matter. During this period, the parties make their final pretrial disclosures of witnesses and exhibits under Federal Rule of Civil Procedure 26(a)(3) [225] and file any motions in limine seeking to exclude or limit testimony or other evidence. A few weeks before the trial is scheduled, the court will hold a final pretrial conference "to formulate a trial plan, including a plan to facilitate the admission of evidence." FED. R. CIV. P. 16(e) [210]. Thereafter, the court will enter a pretrial order, usually prepared jointly by counsel that contains a summary of each party's theory of the case, the issues to be tried, any stipulations of fact, the estimated length of trial, and other matters, depending on the complexity of the case and the preferences of the trial judge.

II. WITNESS AND EXHIBIT LISTS— PRETRIAL DISCLOSURES UNDER RULE 26(a)(3)

Rule 26(a)(3) [225] requires the parties to disclose any evidence they may use at trial. Specifically, each party must (1) name its trial witnesses "separately identifying those the party expects to present and those it may call if the need arises;" (2)

designate any witnesses whose testimony the party expects to present by deposition; and (3) identify each document or other exhibit, "separately identifying those the party expects to offer and those it may offer if the need arises." FED. R. CIV. P. 26(a)(3)(A) [226]. After receiving a party's final pretrial disclosures, the other parties have 14 days to serve and file a list of objections to the use of deposition testimony and the admissibility of documents or other materials designated therein— other than objections based on Federal Rules of Evidence 402 [375] (relevance) and 403 [376] (prejudice). FED. R. CIV. P. 26(a)(3)(B) [229]. Serving and filing a list of objections preserves those objections for trial—the court is not required to rule on the objections. Where appropriate, however, the court may treat an objection as a motion in limine and decide the matter prior to trial. The disclosure and objection process set out in Rule 26(a)(3) [225] expedites the presentation of evidence at trial, often eliminating the need to call witnesses to authenticate documents prior to their admission into evidence. FED. R. CIV. P. 26(a)(3)(B) advisory committee's note (1993) [228].

QUESTIONS

Here are links to the plaintiff Thomas Neely's witness list [414] and exhibit list [413] and defendant Fox of Oak Ridge's witness list [435] and exhibit list [436]. Please review these documents and answer the following questions:

1.   What witnesses did the plaintiff designate?

2. Did the plaintiff separately designate those witnesses he expected to call and those witnesses he might call?

3. Did the plaintiff designate any witnesses whose testimony he expected to present by deposition?

4. What exhibits did the plaintiff designate?

5. Did the plaintiff separately identify the exhibits he expected to offer and those he might offer?

6. What witnesses did the defendant Fox of Oak Ridge designate?

7. Did Fox of Oak Ridge separately designate those witnesses it expected to call and those witnesses it might call?

8. Did Fox of Oak Ridge designate any witnesses whose testimony it expected to present by deposition?

9. What exhibits did Fox of Oak Ridge designate?

10. Did Fox of Oak Ridge separately identify the exhibits it expected to offer and those it might offer?

III. MOTIONS IN LIMINE

Motions in limine—a term derived from the Latin for "threshold"—are motions brought prior to trial to exclude or limit particular testimony or evidence. By enabling the court to hear and rule on evidentiary issues before trial, motions in limine (1) reduce the possibility of the jury hearing inadmissible evidence; (2) cut down on objections and arguments that interrupt the trial proceedings; and (3) allow counsel and the court to give due consideration to evidentiary disputes, rather than objecting and ruling "on the fly." Motions in limine may have a significant impact on the trial, particularly if key evidence is excluded. They may also be used to clear up more simple "housekeeping" matters. In either case, if counsel is aware of an evidentiary issue or dispute, it is better to address it prior to trial with a motion in limine, rather than wait to make an objection in the course of trial.

Motions in limine are not referred to specifically in the Federal Rules of Civil Procedure or Evidence and are governed largely by the practices and procedures set by the individual judge (sometimes referred to as "local, local rules"). For example, the website of the United States District Court for the Eastern District of Tennessee, where *Neely v. Fox* was filed, contains lists of "Judicial Preferences" [480] for most of the judges and magistrate judges that address many topics, including motions in limine. The list of Judicial Preferences for Magistrate Judge Guyton, under the heading "Approach to in limine motions" states, "set by scheduling order." The scheduling order [408] in *Neely v. Fox* required any motions in limine to be filed by June 6, 2006.

Motions in Limine in Neely v. Fox

Three motions in limine were filed in *Neely v. Fox*. The plaintiff filed two: (1) [427] a motion to exclude evidence of any lost wages that had been paid to the plaintiff or medical expenses that had been forgiven or discounted, and (2) [429] a motion to exclude any reference to the fact that he was not wearing a seat belt at the time of the accident. The first motion was based on what is called the "collateral source rule." As the plaintiff explained in his supporting brief:

Under the collateral source rule, the fact that the plaintiffs, in an action for damages in tort, have received payments from a collateral source, other than the defendants, is not admissible in evidence and does not reduce or mitigate the defendant's liability [428].

This may seem like a strange rule that could allow a plaintiff to obtain a double recovery for one set of injuries, but that is normally not the case. The collateral source that made the earlier payment is often an insurance company or other financial institution that is entitled to be repaid by the insured out of any recovery obtained by its insured, the plaintiff. This is called "subrogation" and it means that the insurer stands in the shoes of the insured, as it were.

The plaintiff's second motion was based on TENN. CODE ANN. § 55–9–604(a) [500], which states that in civil actions not involving products liability: "The failure to wear a safety belt or receipt of a citation or warrant for arrest for failure to wear a safety belt shall not be admissible into evidence [429] . . . ." Fox of Oak Ridge did not file a response to either of the plaintiff's motions in limine, and at the pretrial conference counsel, both parties announced they had reached an agreement [431] regarding these motions, and they were granted accordingly.

Fox of Oak Ridge filed a motion in limine to strike testimony regarding the plaintiff's employability from the video deposition of Thomas Koenig, M.D., plaintiff's treating orthopedic surgeon [426]. Fox contended Dr. Koenig was not qualified as an expert to give an opinion regarding whether the plaintiff was capable of employment similar to his former position—which was a psychiatric technician, or capable of employment generally. Fox objected during the deposition that such testimony was beyond Dr. Koenig's expertise [423]. Also, Fox pointed out in its motion in limine that:

> On cross examination, [Dr. Koenig] admitted that he is not qualified as a vocational rehabilitation counselor. (Deposition [423] of Thomas Koenig, M.D., page 35, lines 13–14). He further acknowledged that he has no ability to know what jobs are available for disabled other than a "good general idea." (Deposition of Thomas Koenig, M.D., page 35, lines 17–19). The witness acknowledged that his "general ability" to testify about employability is equal to that of any other board certified orthopedic surgeon, and that he has never performed a vocational analysis. (Deposition of Thomas Koenig, M.D., pages 35–6, lines 20–25, 1, 6) [423].

The plaintiff filed a response to the motion, arguing that Dr. Koenig had not been proffered as an expert in the field of vocational rehabilitation; rather, Dr. Koenig simply testified in his expert capacity as an orthopedic surgeon about Mr. Neely's physical restrictions. (Deposition of Thomas

Koenig, M.D., page 32, lines 1–2) [418]. The plaintiff maintained: "Dr. Koenig's first-hand knowledge regarding Mr. Neely's former job description, which was obtained in the course of over a year by Dr. Koenig's treatment of Mr. Neely. (Deposition of . Thomas Koenig, M.D., page 14, lines 13–20; page 30, lines 22–25, and page 31, lines 1–6) [418], and thus, Dr. Koenig testified concerning his treatment and the physical restrictions, which he placed upon Mr. Neely, and not as a vocational rehabilitation counselor as the Defendant would suggest [403]." The plaintiff also argued that the motion should be denied because Fox had failed to object when Dr. Koenig testified that he did not believe the plaintiff was employable, and thus, Fox had waived this objection [402].

After considering the matter at the pretrial conference [432], the court granted Fox's motion in limine, and struck portions of Dr. Koenig's deposition testimony:

> The Court finds that the defendants properly preserved their objection to Dr. Koenig's testimony regarding the plaintiff's employability. The Court further finds that the plaintiff's general employability is an issue outside of Dr. Koenig's area of expertise as an orthopaedic surgeon. Accordingly, the defendants' motion in limine [Doc. 16] is **GRANTED**. The following testimony shall be stricken from Dr. Koenig's deposition: page 30, line 14 to page 31, line 6, and page 32, lines 10–14 [403]. Dr. Koenig may render an opinion regarding the plaintiff's

anatomical restrictions, and he may testify with regard to any findings that he made with respect to these restrictions and how they relate to the physical requirements of a particular job. However, Dr. Koenig will not be permitted to testify as to the plaintiff's general employability, as that issue is a matter beyond Dr. Koenig's area of expertise [431].

QUESTIONS

Look at the plaintiff's first motion [427] in limine, the brief [428], and his second motion in limine [429] to answer these questions.

1. Why do you think Fox of Oak Ridge did not file responses to the plaintiff's motions in limine?

2. Were the plaintiff's motions in limine necessary?

3. In granting Fox's motion in limine, the court struck the following testimony from Dr. Koenig's deposition: page 30, line 14 to page 31, line 6, and page 32, lines 10–14 [490]. What was the substance of this testimony? How do you think striking this testimony might have affected the plaintiff's case?

IV. FINAL PRE-TRIAL CONFERENCE

The final pretrial conference is held "as close to the start of trial as is reasonable and must be attended by at least one attorney who will conduct the trial for each party . . . ." FED. R. CIV. P. 16(e) [210]. The conference is an important case management tool whose purpose is to "formulate a trial plan, including a plan to facilitate the admission of evidence." FED. R. CIV. P. 16(e) [210]. How this is accomplished depends on the judge and his or her preferences, practices, and procedures for conducting trial. Ideally, the conference enables the judge to ensure that counsel are prepared and know what to expect at the various stages of trial, including choosing a jury, opening statements, direct and cross-examination of witnesses, closing arguments, and instructing the jury on the applicable law. The conference also helps to make sure that counsel and the judge are on the same page regarding the factual and legal issues in the case and affords the judge the opportunity to address any outstanding issues, including motions in limine.

The final pretrial conference [432] in *Neely v. Fox* was held on June 13, 2006. At the conference: (1) counsel for the plaintiff announced he intended to dismiss defendant Benjamin Curd pursuant to Federal Rule of Civil Procedure 41(a) [290];[17] (2) counsel for both parties announced their agreement regarding the plaintiff's motions in limine and those motions were granted by the court; (3) the court granted defendant Fox of Oak Ridge's motion in limine and struck portions of Dr. Koenig's

---

[17] The minute entry from the pretrial conference refers to Rule 4(a). However, Rule 41(a) of the Federal Rules of Civil Procedures covers voluntary dismissals by the plaintiff. A Stipulated Dismissal of Benjamin Curd [459] pursuant to Rule 41(a) was entered "nunc pro tunc" June 15, 2006. Nunc pro tunc is Latin for "now for then" in this case the stipulated dismissal was actually filed on June 21, 2006. Note that Mr. Curd was dismissed "without prejudice"—meaning he could be added again as a defendant if necessary.

deposition testimony; and (4) the court directed the parties to "promptly submit the proposed pretrial order [432]."

QUESTIONS

1. Why does Rule 16(e) [210] call for the final pretrial conference to be held as close to the start of trial as is reasonable?

2. Why are the attorneys who will conduct the trial required to attend the final pretrial conference?

V. THE PRETRIAL ORDER

The pretrial order entered after final pretrial conference controls the subsequent course of the civil action, including trial, and may be modified "only to prevent manifest injustice." FED. R. CIV. P. 16(d) & (e) [209]. The length and complexity of the pre-trial order depends on the nature of the case and the preferences of the judge. In many courts, counsel are directed to jointly prepare the pretrial order and are given instructions on what the order should contain. In *Neely v. Fox*, Magistrate Judge Guyton's instructions regarding the pretrial order were set out in the scheduling order [408].

Pretrial orders often contain: a statement of the basis of subject matter jurisdiction; each party's theory of the case; the issues in dispute; stipulations of fact; lists of each party's witnesses and exhibits; and the estimated length of the trial. The pretrial order [437] in *Neely v. Fox* was simple and straightforward. Here [128] are examples of pretrial orders from other federal courts that were collected in the Federal Judicial Center's Civil Litigation Management Manual, Appendix A. As you can see, they vary in length, content, and complexity.

QUESTIONS

Review the pretrial order [437] in *Neely v. Fox* and answer the following questions:

1. What was the basis for the court's jurisdiction?

2. What was the plaintiff's theory of the case?

3. What was the defendant's theory of the case?

4. What were the issues listed in the pretrial order?

5. Based on your review of the plaintiff's and the defendant's theories of the case, can you think of any issues that might be missing?

6. What stipulations of fact did the pretrial order contain?

7. What was the estimated length of trial?

8. Why do you think the case did not settle before trial?

CHAPTER 9

TRIAL

I. OVERVIEW

If a civil action is not settled in the pre-trial phase, the case is brought to trial and decided by a trier of fact—either a jury, or a judge in what is called a "bench trial." In a jury trial, after the presentation of evidence and arguments by counsel, the jury renders a verdict based on its finding of facts and application of law, which is set out by the court in jury instructions. FED. R. CIV. P. 51 [327]. In a bench trial, the judge renders a decision based on his or her findings of fact and conclusions of law. FED. R. CIV. P. 52(a) [328]. Although many cases settle prior to trial, *Neely v. Fox* did not and proceeded to a two-day jury trial beginning on June 20, 2006 [438].

There are many phases in a civil jury trial: (1) a jury is selected and given preliminary instructions; (2) counsel give their opening statements; (3) the evidence is presented; (4) motions for a judgment as a matter of law may be brought at the close of the plaintiff's or defendant's cases; (5) counsel give closing arguments; (6) the jury is instructed on the law applicable to the case; (7) the jury deliberates and renders a verdict.

II. ASSEMBLING AND SELECTING THE JURY

A. THE JURY POOL

In federal civil actions, potential jurors are selected at random from voter registration lists and/or driver's license lists from the counties within the particular federal district. Potential jurors are sent questionnaires [482] to determine if they are qualified to serve on a jury. To sit on a jury a person must:

- be a United States citizen;

- be at least 18 years old;

- have resided in the judicial district for one year;

- be able to read, write, and understand English well enough to fill out the juror qualification questionnaire;

- have no disqualifying mental or physical condition;

- not currently be charged with a felony; and

- never have been convicted of a felony, unless their civil rights have been legally restored.

28 U.S.C. § 1865(b) [54]. After the juror qualification questionnaires are reviewed, the court randomly selects persons to be summoned for jury duty. 28 U.S.C. § 1866(a) & (b) [55]. Most district court websites have information available for potential jurors such as jury service handbooks and

"frequently asked questions" regarding jury duty. *Neely v. Fox* was filed in the United States District Court for the Eastern District of Tennessee. Jury resources are available on that court's website, currently at http://www.tned.uscourts.gov/juror_index.php.

When a jury is needed for trial, a group of potential jurors is sent to the courtroom where the trial will take place. Counsel then select the jury from this group through a process called voir dire.

B. VOIR DIRE

The jury in a federal civil action must have at least six members who, unless the parties stipulate otherwise, must all participate in deliberations and render a unanimous verdict. FED. R. CIV. P. 48(a) & (b) [303]. As a practical matter, many courts empanel more than the minimum six jurors in case one or more jurors must be excused during the trial or deliberations. In *Neely v. Fox*, eight jurors were selected.

Voir dire, Anglo-French for "to speak the truth," is the process by which the jury is selected—where potential jurors are questioned by the judge, counsel, or both to determine if they are suitable to serve on the jury. If the court examines potential jurors, it must permit counsel "to make any further inquiry it considers proper, or must itself ask any of their additional questions it considers proper." FED. R. CIV. P. 47(a) [302].

First and foremost voir dire is used to screen for potential jurors who may not be able to judge the case fairly and impartially—because they know any person involved in the case, have information about the case, or have biases about the people or issues involved in the case. If a potential juror is shown to have a connection to the case or persons involved or to be biased, he or she will be excused—either on the court's initiative or through a challenge "for cause" made by counsel. 28 U.S.C. § 1870 [56]. In addition to determining whether potential jurors are suitable, counsel for the parties use voir dire to determine which jurors are the most and least desirable. To that end, in federal civil actions each side is allowed at least three "peremptory challenges," in which counsel does not have to state a reason for excusing the potential juror. 28 U.S.C. § 1870 [56]. However, no person may be excluded from a jury "on account of race, color, religion, sex, national origin, or economic status." 28 U.S.C. § 1862 [53].[18] Therefore, peremptory challenges may not be used to exclude potential jurors based solely on these criteria. *See Edmonson v. Leesville Concrete Co., Inc.*, 500 U.S. 614, 616 (1991) [107].

C. VOIR DIRE IN *NEELY V. FOX*

Voir dire in *Neely v. Fox* began with Judge Guyton administering an oath to the jury pool, briefly explaining the jury selection process, and

---

[18] As of this writing, a bill was pending in Congress to add sexual orientation as another category of prohibited discriminatory criteria.

outlining the subject matter of the case [582]. Eight
potential jurors were called and seated in the jury
box [584], and Judge Guyton asked them
preliminary questions regarding (1) prior knowledge
regarding the case or familiarity with counsel or the
parties; (2) prior jury service or involvement in civil
or criminal actions; (3) reasons they might have that
would affect their ability to be impartial; and (4) any
physical problems that might affect their ability to
serve on the jury [583]. After his preliminary
questions, Judge Guyton found the initial eight
potential jurors to be qualified to serve on the jury
[595].

Counsel were then allowed to question the eight
potential jurors directly. Robert English, the
plaintiff's counsel, went first. After confirming that
all eight jurors could drive, Mr. English asked if any
of them had been involved in a personal injury suit:

MR. ENGLISH: Have any of you ever been
involved in a personal injury lawsuit arising out
of any kind of personal injury, whether you sued
someone or someone sued you? Mr. (Juror 137),
you held your hand up?

JUROR NO. 137 [598]: Yeah, my boy was
[around his graduation, he was going to school
and drifted over the lane divider line and hit an
officer—I got sued for $300,000].

Mr. English asked follow-up questions of Juror No.
137, during which he indicated his reluctance and
discomfort with sitting on the jury in the case [597].

As a result, Mr. English moved to have Juror No. 137 excused, a request that the court granted [597].

Another juror was called in place of Juror No. 137 and Judge Guyton asked her the same types of preliminary questions as he had the others [599].

Mr. English then resumed his questioning— exploring whether there would be any reason why any of the eight potential jurors might not be able to be follow the law or be impartial in the case [600]. Mr. English did not make any challenges for cause, and thereafter, Clint Woodfin, counsel for the defendant began his questions [602].

Mr. Woodfin asked if any of the eight potential jurors had been involved in a car accident or had had any trouble with their back or neck [601]. Juror No. 23 indicated that he had had two disks removed and three vertebrae fused in his back as the result of a helicopter accident in Vietnam [603]. In answering Mr. Woodfin's follow up questions, Juror No. 23 revealed that he was not sure he could be fair if pain was an element in the case:

JUROR 23: I spent two tours in Vietnam, and I have seen a lot of pain, stuff. I don't know. I'd love to hear the case and I would like to make—I would like to be able to pass judgment on it, but I'm awful afraid that if you really prove that there's a lot of pain involved in this, then that's going to persuade me, I can tell you now. I'm just telling you, I guess; okay?

MR. WOODFIN: I appreciate your candidness about that. Do you think that this particular case and what you've heard about it so far may not be the best case for you to sit on, considering what testimony you're probably going to hear about what Mr. Neely claims, and also your own situation?

JUROR NO. 23: I think so. I don't want to be unfair to the folks in the case, and I'm not sure that I can't be if there's a lot of pain involved in this [604].

The judge then excused Juror No. 23, and another juror was called in his place [605]. At the same time, Juror No. 4 volunteered that he thought there were too many lawsuits and he did not think he could be fair and impartial based on that [607]. As a result, Juror No. 4 [608] was also excused and another juror was called.

Mr. Woodfin and Mr. English asked additional questions of the potential jurors, but did not make any more challenges for cause [606]. Three jurors, however, were excused based on peremptory challenges [611]. Three new jurors were called in their place and were questioned by the court and counsel [610]. Of these three jurors, one was excused based on a peremptory challenge [612]. Eventually one more potential juror was excused for cause [613] and another based on a peremptory challenge [614] before a jury was selected and sworn in. In total, nine potential jurors were excused during voir dire—four for cause [596], and five based on peremptory challenges [609].

QUESTIONS

Review the portions of the *Neely v. Fox* trial transcript in which potential jurors were excused for cause [596] and answer the following questions:

1. Which jurors were excused based on a motion by counsel?

2. If the defendant's counsel had not moved to excuse Juror 23, do you think the plaintiff's counsel would have? Why or why not?

3. Which juror was dismissed based on his own and the court's initiative? Why was this juror excused?

4. Which juror was excused on the court's initiative after asking preliminary questions? Why was this juror excused?

5. Do you agree with the court's decision to excuse this juror?

Review the portions of the *Neely v. Fox* trial transcript in which potential jurors were excused based on peremptory challenges and answer the following questions:

6. Which jurors were excused based on peremptory challenges?

7. Which attorney challenged which jurors?

8. Why were the peremptory challenges made by filling out a form rather than in open court like the challenges for cause?

9. Why do you think Juror No. 7 may have been excused based on a peremptory challenge?

10. Why do you think Juror No. 6 may have been excused based on a peremptory challenge?

III. PRELIMINARY JURY INSTRUCTIONS

After the jury in a civil action is empanelled and sworn in, the court gives preliminary jury instructions regarding the jurors' role, trial procedure, and pertinent issues in the case before them. Most judges have a standard set of preliminary jury instructions that they tailor to the individual case.

In *Neely v. Fox*, Judge Guyton began by explaining the jurors' role in deciding the facts and his role in deciding questions of law:

All right. Members of the jury, welcome again to jury service in federal court. Now that you have been sworn as a jury to try this case, the Court will give you some preliminary instructions on your proper role and conduct as members of the jury.

As the jury, you have an important responsibility to decide what the facts are that are in dispute in this case. As the judge, I will decide all questions of law and procedure from time to time during the trial, and at the end of the trial I will instruct you on the rules of law that you must follow in making your decision.

You, the members of the jury, will decide what the facts are from the evidence that will be presented in court. You and you alone are the judges of the facts. You will hear the evidence, decide what the facts are, and then apply the law I give you to those facts. You must follow the law which I give you whether you agree with it or not. That is how you will reach your verdict [616].

Judge Guyton also explained how the trial would proceed:

> The evidence will consist of the testimony of the witnesses, all documents and other tangible things received into evidence as exhibits, and any facts that the lawyers agree on or that I instruct you should accept as being true.
>
> In a moment the lawyers for each of the parties will make what is called an opening statement. This will be a summary of the evidence each party plans to present in court. It is designed to give you a general idea of what this case is about. What the lawyers say in their opening statements is not evidence.
>
> After the lawyers' opening statements, the parties will present their evidence. The person who brings the lawsuit is called the plaintiff. A plaintiff always seeks some relief against the other party, called the defendant. A plaintiff alleges that the defendant in some manner was at fault and that as a result of this the plaintiff suffered a loss.
>
> The Plaintiff goes first, calling his witnesses and putting his exhibits into evidence. Then the Defendant puts on its witnesses and exhibits. After that, the Plaintiff may present rebuttal proof. Then the lawyers will again address you for closing arguments. After that,

you will be sent to the jury room to decide on your verdict [617].

Judge Guyton also discussed the burden of proof in a civil action as opposed to a criminal case:

I want to talk to you briefly about the burden of proof. In a civil action such as this one, in order to recover money damages, the Plaintiff must prove his claims by a preponderance of the evidence. That means the Plaintiff has to produce evidence which, considered in the light of all the facts, leads you to believe that what the Plaintiff claims is more likely true than not.

To put it differently, if you were to put the Plaintiff's and the Defendant's evidence on opposite sides of the scales, the Plaintiff's evidence would have to make the scales tip somewhat on the Plaintiff's side. If the Plaintiff fails to meet this burden, the verdict must be for the Defendant.

Those of you who have sat on criminal cases will have heard the term "proof beyond a reasonable doubt." That requirement does not apply to a civil case such as this one, and you should therefore please put that concept out of your mind [618].

Then Judge Guyton briefly instructed the jury on the issues of negligence and legal causation which the plaintiff had the burden of proving at trial:

I want to talk to you about the law that applies in this case just briefly. I will give you detailed instructions at the end of this trial, and those instructions will govern your deliberations. However, in order to help you follow the evidence you are about to hear, I will give you at this time a brief summary of the elements which the Plaintiff must prove in order to make out his case.

A plaintiff is entitled to recover compensation for an injury that was legally caused by the negligent conduct of the defendant. In this case, the Plaintiff has the burden of proving that the [Defendant] was at fault. In this case, this means the Plaintiff has the burden of proving that the Defendant was negligent and that the negligence was a legal cause of injury to the Plaintiff.

Negligence is the failure to use reasonable care. It is either doing something that a reasonably careful person would not do or failing to do something that a reasonably careful person would do under circumstances similar to those shown by the evidence. A person may assume that every other person will use reasonable care unless the circumstances indicate the contrary to a reasonably careful person.

The second part of fault is what I just mentioned, legal cause. A legal cause of an injury is a cause which, in natural and continuous sequence, produces an injury and without which the injury would not have occurred. A single injury can be caused by the negligent acts or omissions of one or more persons.

If you find that a party was negligent and that the negligence was a legal cause of the injury or damages for which claim was made, you have found that party to be at fault. The Plaintiff has the burden to prove the Defendant's fault. If the Plaintiff fails to do so, you should find no fault on the part of the Defendant [619].

Judge Guyton concluded his preliminary instructions by admonishing the jurors not to talk about the case with anyone else, not to read or listen to reports about the case from any media, and not to do any independent investigation regarding the case, including Internet research [620].

QUESTIONS

1. According to the judge's instructions, what was the jury's role in the case? What was the court's role?

2. Why do you think Judge Guyton contrasted the burden of proof in a civil action with that in a criminal action?

3. Since Judge Guyton would instruct the jury in detail regarding the law to apply, why did he give preliminary instructions on the legal elements negligence and causation?

IV. OPENING STATEMENTS

In their opening statements counsel for the plaintiff and counsel for the defendant present their theory of the case—focusing on the facts of the case as opposed to legal argument. Counsel for the plaintiff goes first and usually describes the case in terms of what he or she intends to prove. In response, counsel for the defendant will often discuss weaknesses in the plaintiff's case, attempting to plant doubt in the jury's mind regarding as many issues as possible.

Here is how Robert English, counsel for the plaintiff, Thomas Neely, began his opening statement:

Ladies and gentlemen, two years ago, on a warm, hot July day, Tom Neely's life was changed forever. He was going to work, going to work to a job that he loved at the Ridgeview Psychiatric Facility. Been working there for a year and a half.

He lived in Kentucky, drove near 100 miles to work one way, because he loved the job and it was the best job he had ever had. He had worked at Scott County Hospital for about 12 years, security and orderly, doing hard work.

Security work requires you to stand up and to walk nine to five. Being an orderly, most of you have had healthcare experience knows what that entails. It entails lifting. It's a hard job. His job as a psychiatric technician who was working and where he was going the day of this accident required him to be able to stand on his feet, lift 75 pounds, to subdue unruly clients or patients that really might have hurt themselves.

This was his job and this was his chosen profession. This is what he had done for a year and a half. This is a job that he drove 100 miles one way each day to do because he loved it [621].

Mr. English then briefly described accident in which the defendant's employee rear-ended the plaintiff while driving on a rain-slick road [622]. Mr. English focused his opening statement on the injuries plaintiff alleged were the result of the accident, their treatment by physicians, and their affect on the plaintiff's life and ability to work [623]. Mr. English concluded:

So that's our case. I think it's a very simple case. We haven't sued for property damage. That's already—that's been resolved. So the only thing we're suing for now is for the damages that this— and the effect that these damages had on Tom.

We ask you to listen carefully and give us adequate compensation. Thank you [624].

Clint Woodfin, counsel for the defendant, Fox of Oak Ridge, began his opening statement by reminding the jurors that opening statements are not evidence and then focused on the burden of proof:

Good afternoon, everybody. Thank you for being patient in listening to us as we make these opening statements regarding what we think the evidence is going to prove in this case. Judge Guyton will tell you also, what we say to you here is not evidence. It's our role as an advocate for our client, and also is a role as an advocate for the legal system itself.

. . .

You understand, as we've talked about during the initial meetings that we've had, that the Plaintiff has the burden of proving all of these things to you by that preponderance of the evidence standard. The Defendant, Mr. Fox and I, we don't have to prove anything. We don't even have to put any evidence on.

But what we do is take a look at their evidence and bring out points which reflect against the weight of that evidence. And after doing that in this case, it's my opinion that it's very clear that the Plaintiff has not met his burden of proving these things by any measure whatsoever [625].

Mr. Woodfin spent a brief time discussing whether Fox's employee, Benjamin Curd, had been negligent in causing the accident. He spent the majority of his opening statement disputing that "Mr. Neely sustained damages that are directly a result of what happened in that accident [626]." He concluded as follows:

Our system works real well when the jurors listen to the evidence and listen to the instructions that the Court gives, and I suspect you're going to do that today.

I want to thank you all for taking the time to be here and listening to what we have to say about it and letting us present the case and letting me present the case on behalf of Fox of Oak Ridge so that you can truly understand what's going on here. We'll try to present this as clearly and concisely as possible so you can get to the point where you can help us decide these issues. Thank you [627].

QUESTIONS

1. Why do you think counsel for the plaintiff began his opening statement by focusing on the job the plaintiff had at the time of the accident?

2. Why do you think counsel for the defendant began his opening statement by reminding the jury that opening statements are not evidence and focusing on the burden of proof?

3. Based on your review of the opening statements [581] of plaintiff's counsel and defendant's counsel, what do you think will be the central issue in dispute at trial?

V. PRESENTING THE EVIDENCE

A. OVERVIEW

The core of a civil trial is the presentation of the evidence, which, as Judge Guyton explained, consists of testimony by witnesses—including the parties; documents and other tangible things that are admitted as exhibits; and any stipulations of fact by the parties that are read to the jury. Evidence presented at trial must be relevant, meaning that: "(a) it has any tendency to make a fact more or less probable than it would be without the evidence; and (b) the fact is of consequence in determining the action." FED. R. EVID. 401 [374]. At trial plaintiffs present their evidence first in what is often called the "case in chief." Then defendants may, but do not have to, present evidence in their defense, after which the plaintiff may present evidence in rebuttal.

The Federal Rules of Civil Procedure state a preference for testimony of witnesses to be taken live in court consistent with the hearsay rule.[19] FED. R. CIV. P. 43 [292]. However, witness testimony may be presented by deposition under certain circumstances, including where the witness is unavailable at trial, or where the parties and the court agree. FED. R. CIV. P. 32 [256]. Counsel must specifically designate those witnesses whose testimony they expect to present by deposition in their pretrial disclosures. FED. R. CIV. P. 26(a)(3)(A)(ii) [227]. In *Neely v. Fox*, the plaintiff's witness list noted that video deposition testimony would be used for Joe Browder, M.D. and Thomas Koenig, M.D. [414]

When testimony is presented live in court, the witness takes the stand, swears or affirms to tell the truth, and then counsel for the party who called the witness conducts a "direct examination." In the direct examination counsel ask questions of the witness designed to elicit testimony that will support their theory of the case or defense. After the direct examination is complete, opposing counsel has an opportunity for "cross-examination." During

[19] Hearsay consists of a statement that: (1) the declarant does not make while testifying at the current trial or hearing; and (2) a party offers to prove the truth of the matter asserted in the statement. Under the hearsay rule, this evidence is generally not admissible, although there are many exceptions to this rule. *See* FED. R. EVID. 801–804 [381].

cross-examination, counsel attempt to (1) undermine or lessen the impact of the witness' direct testimony, and (2) elicit testimony that is damaging to the other side. After a witness is cross-examined, counsel who called the witness may conduct a "redirect examination" to attempt to explain or minimize potentially damaging testimony that came out in cross-examination.

B. PRESENTATION OF EVIDENCE IN *NEELY V. FOX*

1. Stipulations of Fact

The presentation of the evidence began with Judge Guyton reading the parties' stipulations of fact to the jury—in particular, that on the day of the accident, Benjamin Curd was operating a Chevrolet Van as the defendant's agent [628].

2. The Plaintiff's Case in Chief

The plaintiff's case in chief consisted of four witnesses—the plaintiff, Thomas Neely, and Drs. Joe Browder and Thomas Koenig by video deposition; and ten exhibits that were introduced during the plaintiff's direct examination—pictures of plaintiff's damaged Kia and the accident scene, plaintiff's tax returns, and documents showing his medical expenses.

Direct Examination of the Plaintiff

The first witness was the plaintiff, Thomas Neely, and Robert English conducted the direct examination. Mr. English asked preliminary

questions about the plaintiff and his family—a wife
and two children ages 2 ½ and 7 months—and then
elicited testimony about the plaintiff's prior jobs as
a hospital security guard and a psychiatric
technician [629]. In particular, Mr. Neely testified
regarding the physical demands of those positions
and that he was no longer able to perform them in
his present condition [630].

Mr. English also took Mr. Neely through the
events leading to the accident. Mr. Neely testified
that it was raining and that he slowed to almost a
complete stop because the car in front of him was
turning into a business center and had to slow to
almost a stop in order to drive over a large hump in
the road [631]. Mr. Neely had measured the hump
at Mr. English's request, and found it to be 7 inches
high [632]. He could see the van that hit him in his
rear view mirror and "knew he wasn't going to be
able to stop [586]." Mr. Neely testified: "After the
impact I was slung forward, and then my seatbelt
caught me, and I was ejected backwards, and I
ended up in the back seat after the seat broke, and I
was laying in a flat position, looking up at the top of
the car [587]." He testified further that his car had
been "totaled" in the accident [588].

Mr. English then focused his direct examination
on the plaintiff's injuries and inability to work. Mr.
English first elicited testimony that Mr. Neely had
weighed the same, 300 pounds, before the accident
and had been able to work as a hospital security
guard and psychiatric technician [589]. Mr. Neely
testified that he was transported by ambulance to a

local hospital where they took X-rays, performed a C.T. scan, and released him with the proviso that he follow up with his family doctor the next day [590].

Mr. Neely testified that he went to several doctors, including Dr. Koenig, an orthopedic surgeon, who was among a list of doctors recommended by his attorney, Michael Inman. Mr. Neely underwent physical therapy; MRI (magnetic resonance imaging) scans were performed on his neck and back; TENS (transcutaneous electrical nerve stimulation) was prescribed; and Dr. Koenig referred him to Dr. Joe Browder, a pain specialist who prescribed methadone [591].

Mr. Neely stated that he continued to be in considerable pain, had not worked since the accident, although he had applied for jobs at Kroger and Wal-Mart and helped his wife sell things at flea markets and watched the children, and that his pain and mobility problems significantly limited his daily activity [593]. Mr. Neely's tax return for 2003 indicated he had earned $19,280 [594].

The direct examination of Mr. Neely resumed the next day, when he testified that as a result of the accident, he was behind on his bills. He stated that he had never before had a problem paying his bills and had worked continuously at one job or another since he was 13 [523].

Cross Examination of the Plaintiff

Clint Woodfin, counsel for the defendant, began his cross examination by questioning Mr. Neely about his measuring the hump in the road "[d]espite

the fact that you can't do anything [546]." Then Mr.
Woodfin assailed the plaintiff's credibility by going
over apparent discrepancies between Mr. Neely's
prior deposition testimony and what he had
reported to his doctors or had just testified to on
direct examination [550].

Then Mr. Woodfin questioned Mr. Neely
regarding his ability to work and lift items under 15
pounds and a worker's compensation case involving
Mr. Neely in which he'd injured his knee [512]. Mr.
Woodfin also tried to make the point that the
doctors who were going to testify for Mr. Neely had
been referred to him by his lawyers [513].

In addition, Mr. Woodfin elicited testimony from
Mr. Neely that he did not know how long the van
had been traveling behind him or anything about
the speed at which it was traveling [514]. Mr.
Woodfin concluded his cross examination by having
Mr. Neely describe how he drove his car home after
the accident [515].

Redirect Examination of the Plaintiff

On redirect, Mr. English questioned Mr. Neely
about what physical movement was involved in
measuring the hump in the road, the fact that the
impact broke the seat of Mr. Neely's car, what Dr.
Koenig had focused on in treating him, his search
for employment, his worker's compensation case,
and the personal belongings he and his wife had
sold at flea markets [516].

Video Depositions of Drs. Joe Browder and Thomas Koenig

In the next phase of the plaintiff's case, his counsel played the video recorded depositions of Dr. Joe Browder, who treated the plaintiff's pain, and Dr. Thomas Koenig, plaintiff's orthopedic surgeon. The court explained to the jury that testimony by video was fairly common with medical professionals, and stated: "You should consider this testimony that's being given by videotape to be just as if it were being given here in the courtroom. Give it the same weight as you would any testimony that would be given in the courtroom [517]."

Because the deposition testimony of Dr. Browder was not part of a motion or other filing in *Neely v. Fox,* the transcript was not filed with the court. The deposition testimony of Dr. Koenig, however, had been the subject of a motion in limine, and thus it is part of the record and can be viewed here [423]. Remember that page 30, lines 14 to page 31, line 6 and page 32, lines 10–14 [490] were stricken by the court in granting the defendant's motion in limine [431]. *See* Chapter 8, Section III, p. 107.

On direct examination in the deposition, Mr. English took Dr. Koenig through his diagnosis, treatment, and assessment of the plaintiff's injuries and impairment as a result of the accident. After conducting MRI and C-T scans, Dr. Koenig diagnosed Mr. Neely with lumbrosacral and cervical strains with "tearing of ligaments" that he likened to severe ankle sprain. He also noted that Mr.

Neely had preexisting congenital disc disease that
was made worse by the accident [422].

Dr. Koenig testified that in his estimation, Mr.
Neely had an 8% permanent cervical impairment
prior to the accident and 22% impairment after the
accident—meaning the accident had caused an
added 14% permanent cervical impairment. Dr.
Koenig testified that Mr. Neely had an 8% lumbar
impairment as a result of the accident and that he
had reached maximum improvement [417],
meaning: "We don't think he's going to get much
worse, we don't think he's going to get much better."
Dr. Koenig explained that conservative and semi-
conservative treatment such as physical therapy
and anti-inflamatories were not successful in
relieving the pain Mr. Neely complained of [416].

In November 2005 at Mr. Neely's last
appointment, Dr. Koenig gave him a permanent "no
duty" status, meaning the doctor "didn't really think
he could do anything [418]." In July 2005, however,
Dr. Koenig had given Mr. Neely a limited duty
status, with restrictions regarding "repetitive
bending, stooping, squatting, or lifting greater than
15 pounds [418]."

In his cross examination Mr. Woodfin focused on
Mr. Neely's prior condition of degenerative disc
disease, the subjective nature of Mr. Neely's
complaints of pain, and that the results of Dr.
Koenig's range of motion tests were based on how
far Mr. Neely said he could go and that there was no
way to measure his effort [419]. Mr. Woodfin also
elicited testimony from Dr. Koenig that although

Mr. Neely had told him he lost consciousness at the time of the accident, Mr. Neely told personnel at the emergency room that he had not [420].

Mr. Woodfin pressed Dr. Koenig to explain what was the change in Mr. Neely from July 2005 to November 2005 that had caused the doctor to change his status from limited duty to no duty. In response, Dr. Koenig testified that he had tried to get Mr. Neely back to the work place "with attempts at weight loss, with attempts of trials of epidural steroids . . . physical therapy . . . despite all those attempts he reports back to me on the 15th of November that he has unchanged low back pain, unchanged neck pain. . . . There comes a time when you have to fish or cut bait [421]."

After Dr. Koenig's deposition was played for the jury, plaintiff's counsel, Robert English, read from the Tennessee Code's Mortality Tables that "Someone who is 48 like Mr. Neely, has a life expectancy of 32.85 years [518]."

Defendant's Motion for Judgment as a Matter of Law

Once a party has been fully heard on an issue in a jury trial, if "the court finds that a reasonable jury would not have a legally sufficient evidentiary basis to find for the party on that issue, the court may . . . resolve the issue against the party[.]" In addition, the court may order judgment as a matter of law against that party on a claim or defense that under controlling law could prevail "only with a favorable finding on that issue." FED. R. CIV. P. 50(a)(1) [324].

A motion for judgment as a matter of law may be brought any time before the case is submitted to the jury, and may be renewed after the jury has rendered a verdict. FED. R. CIV. P. 50(a)(2) [324] & (b) [326].[20]

In *Neely v. Fox*, after the plaintiff rested his case, defense counsel, Clint Woodfin, brought a motion for judgment as a matter of law, which he referred to as a motion for "order directing the verdict in favor of Fox of Oak Ridge [520]." Mr. Woodfin argued there had been no proof that the driver, Benjamin Curd, had been negligent in any manner—only that he hit Mr. Neely from behind, which he maintained was not sufficient [519]. Mr. English responded that it was a "question for the jury to determine who the cause of this accident was [521]." The court agreed, and after hearing further argument from Mr. Woodfin, stated: "I think your argument is that their case is weak. But it's still a jury question. So, respectfully, your motion will be denied [522]."

3. The Defense

For the defense's case, Mr. Woodfin called the driver of the van, Benjamin Curd, and read aloud portions of the plaintiff's deposition testimony.

---

[20] Prior to 1991 if the motion was brought before the case went to the jury it was called a motion for "direction of verdict" or "directed verdict." If the motion was renewed after a verdict was rendered it was called a "motion for judgment notwithstanding the verdict." FED. R. CIV. P. 50 1991 Advisory Committee Notes [325].

Direct and Cross Examination of Benjamin Curd

In his direct examination, Mr. Woodfin asked Mr. Curd about his job at Fox of Oak Ridge and took him through the accident [524]. Mr. Curd testified that it was raining and he was driving slower than the speed limit, and that Mr. Neely "stopped and was on the phone. And before I could stop, I slid into him [526]." Mr. Curd said the impact was not hard, but that Mr. Neely was "leaning back in the car, but the seat went all the way down. It was down, but it was not all the way [527]." Mr. Curd then called an ambulance [527].

In his cross-examination Mr. English elicited testimony from Mr. Curd that the van was a very heavy vehicle and that he was traveling 20 feet behind the plaintiff at 35 miles per hours on a wet road [528]. Mr. Curd also acknowledged that "if he had been following a little further back [he] probably would not have hit [Mr. Neely]," and further that "if [he] had been following a little slower [he] probably wouldn't have hit him [529]." Mr. Curd also agreed that Mr. Neely's seat broke in the accident and that he saw Mr. Neely "looking up at the ceiling of his car [530]."

The Plaintiff's Motion for a Judgment as a Matter of Law

After Mr. Curd was excused, Mr. English moved for a judgment as a matter of law (which he referred to as a directed verdict) in favor of the plaintiff on the issue of negligence. The court denied the motion holding the issue of whether Mr. Curd was negligent was a "jury question [531]."

Mr. Woodfin then read aloud portions of Mr. Neely's deposition testimony and rested his case [532].

QUESTIONS

1. Why do you think Federal Rule of Civil Procedure 43 [292] states a preference for live, in-court testimony?

2. Review the direct examination of the plaintiff [585]. Which portions to you find the most compelling? Which portions do you find the least?

3. Review the cross examination of Mr. Neely [562]. What points do you think Mr. Woodfin was trying to make?

4. Review the transcript of Dr. Koenig's deposition testimony [423]. Do you think this deposition was helpful or hurtful to Mr. Neely, or both? Explain.

5. Review the testimony of Benjamin Curd, the defense witness. Do you think his testimony was helpful or hurtful to the defense, or both? Explain.

VI. CLOSING ARGUMENTS

A. OVERVIEW

Closing arguments are the last opportunity for counsel to address the jurors before they are instructed on the law and sent to deliberate. At that point in the trial, the jury has seen and heard the evidence, and counsel will highlight key portions that support their case and undermine that of the other side. The goal of counsel in closing argument is to persuade the jury to adopt their particular interpretation of the facts—that the facts meet or fail to meet the applicable law. In closing argument, plaintiff's counsel has the first and last word. He or she gives an initial closing argument, followed by the closing argument of the defense counsel, and then has an opportunity for rebuttal.

B.   CLOSING ARGUMENTS IN *NEELY V. FOX*

In *Neely v. Fox* the parties each were allotted 30 minutes for closing argument that could be divided among attorneys [533].

Michael Inman, who was co-counsel for the plaintiff, went first. Mr. Inman introduced himself as the attorney who had referred the plaintiff to Drs. Browder and Koenig, and said it was one of his first jury trials [534]. Mr. Inman briefly went over the accident, pointing to Mr. Curd's testimony that, essentially, "he was going too fast, too close, on too slick a road [538]." Mr. Inman pointed out that Mr. Woodfin could have had a doctor of his choice evaluate Mr. Neely but chose not to [536] do so. He discussed Mr. Neely's injuries and argued that he was unemployable, could not provide for his family, and could not participate in most of the activities he had enjoyed prior to the accident [537]. Then Mr. Inman addressed Mr. Neely's monetary damages for medical bills and loss of past and future wages, as

well as damages for pain and suffering and loss of
enjoyment of life [539]. He concluded by saying
"[W]e're asking you to do what's right and what's
just, and come back with a verdict for Mr. Neely
[541]."

In Mr. Woodfin's closing argument [540] he
likened the plaintiff's case to a "house of cards"—the
most important part being the base. He stated: "In
this case the base on which the whole case is built is
Mr. Neely and him telling these things to doctors
[543]" that Mr. Woodfin argued were not credible. If
the jury determined that Mr. Curd, the driver of the
van, was negligent, Mr. Woodfin said the next
question was whether "this conduct was the cause of
all these things that Mr. Neely has told you about
today. I know the answer to that question, I think
you do too [551]." Mr. Woodfin concluded by
arguing that on the day of the accident "and the
days that followed, [Mr. Neely] decided, I'm not
going to live my life anymore like I used to. I'm
going to try to get money out of this lawsuit. Don't
reward him for that [545]."

Robert English handled rebuttal closing
argument [544] for the plaintiff. He argued that
even though the defendant's employee had followed
Mr. Neely "too closely, too fast, on a rain slick road"
the defendant still had "put this man [Mr. Neely]
through hell for the last two years" even though
most rear end collisions are settled [509]. He
reminded the jury of the MRIs that had shown
injuries to Mr. Neely's neck and back [547] and went
over the testimony of Drs. Browder and Koenig that

Mr. Neely was unable to work. Mr. English pointed out that Mr. Neely had worked since he was 13 and had a job he loved at the time of the accident, but that they would not take him back because he was on methadone for pain and had lifting restrictions [548]. Mr. English closed by reviewing all of Mr. Neely's claimed damages [549].

QUESTIONS

1. Review the closing argument on behalf of the plaintiff given by Michael Inman [535] and the closing argument by his co-counsel, Robert English. Is the tone of the arguments similar or different? What might account for the similarity or difference in tone?

2. Review the closing argument by Mr. Woodfin. Do you think the house of cards analogy was persuasive?

VII. JURY INSTRUCTIONS AND VERDICT FORMS

A. OVERVIEW

Before beginning deliberations, jurors are instructed by the court on the law applicable to the case and how the jury should conduct itself in reaching a verdict. Many courts use pattern jury instructions, with the parties supplying any special requests for particular instructions. *See* FED. R. CIV. P. 51 [327]. Jury instructions are usually read aloud to the jury and printed copies of the instructions are not taken into the jury room. The jury may ask to have particular instructions reread to them, however, as their deliberations play out.

In addition, the court may provide the jury with a verdict form containing questions on specific issues for the jury to answer. FED. R. CIV. P. 49(b) [306]. The questions are set out in order, somewhat like a flow chart, and are designed to lead to a verdict. If a verdict form with questions is used, the court must also give the jury "instructions and explanations necessary to enable the jury to render a general verdict and answer the questions in writing." FED. R. CIV. P. 49(b)(1) [307].

B.   JURY INSTRUCTIONS [575] IN *NEELY V. FOX*

Judge Guyton began by instructing the jury that it was their duty to follow the law as stated in the instructions and "to perform this duty without any bias or prejudice to any party [577]." Judge Guyton then set out the specific issues to be decided:

Number one, was the defendant, Fox of Oak Ridge, negligent?

Number two, was the defendant, Fox of Oak Ridge's, negligence a legal cause of the injuries to the plaintiff Thomas Neely?

Number three, if so, what is the total amount of compensatory damages that the plaintiff Thomas Neely is entitled to recover [564]?

Before setting out the law applicable to these issues, he instructed the jury on the burden of proof—a preponderance of evidence, direct and circumstantial evidence, impeachment, and judging the credibility of the witnesses and the weight of their testimony [563]. Judge Guyton instructed the jury that the plaintiff had the burden of proving that the defendant was at fault, which meant proving the defendant was negligent and that the negligence was the legal cause of his injuries. He explained:

> Negligence is the failure to use reasonable care. It is either doing something that a reasonably careful person would not do, or the failure to do something that a reasonably careful person would do under circumstances similar to those shown by the evidence.
>
> . . .
>
> The second part of fault is legal cause. A legal cause of an injury is a cause which in natural and continuous sequence produces an injury, and without which the injury would not have occurred. A single injury can be caused by a negligent act or omission of one or more persons.
>
> If you find that a party was negligent, and that the negligence was a legal cause of the injury or damages for which a claim was made, you have found that party to be at fault [565].

Judge Guyton also instructed the verdict on "negligence per se" in which a person who violates a statute or ordinance is negligent, but is not at fault unless the jury also found that the violation was a legal cause of the injury or damage [566]. In *Neely v. Fox*, the plaintiff had alleged that Fox's employee, Benjamin Curd had violated TENN. CODE ANN. § 55–8–124(a) [501]—Following too closely.

Regarding damages, Judge Guyton instructed the jury that if it found in favor of the plaintiff it should assess damages that would reasonably compensate him for "the following elements of loss or harm, if any, that he has suffered or will suffer, as a legal result of the fault of the defendant:" past and future physical pain and suffering; past and future mental or emotional pain and suffering; past and future medical expenses; past and future lost earnings; and permanent injury [558].

QUESTIONS

Review the jury instructions in *Neely v. Fox* regarding proving fault [557] and answer the following questions:

1. What two elements did the plaintiff have to prove in order to show that the defendant was at fault?

2. How is negligence defined in the jury instructions?

3. How is legal cause defined in the jury instructions?

C. VERDICT FORM IN *NEELY V. FOX*

A verdict form [167] with written questions was used in *Neely v. Fox* that was approved by both parties and the court. Before the jury was sent to deliberate, Judge Guyton explained:

This is the verdict form. It has three questions.

The first question is: Was the defendant, Fox of Oak Ridge, Inc., negligent?

You will either answer yes or no to that question.

If your answer is no, you simply have your foreperson sign the form and return it to the court.

If your answer is yes, you go to number two: Was the defendant Fox of Oak Ridge, Inc.'s negligence a legal cause of injuries to the plaintiff Thomas Neely?

If your answer to that question is yes, you'll go to the third question which is: What is the total amount of compensatory damages that the plaintiff Thomas Neely is entitled to recover?

Whatever your verdict is, it must be signed and dated by the foreperson of the jury and it must state that your decision must be unanimous [556].

QUESTIONS

1. Review the verdict form [167] and the instructions [556] given above regarding the form. Are there any differences between them? Explain.

2. What are the differences in the instructions set out after Question 1 in the verdict form and the instructions set out after Question 2?

VIII. RENDERING A VERDICT

A. OVERVIEW

All the jurors must participate in deliberations and rendering a verdict and, unless the parties stipulate otherwise, the verdict must be unanimous. FED. R. CIV. P. 48 [304]. Jury deliberations are conducted in private, out of the hearing of the judge, court staff, the attorneys, parties, witnesses, etc. Thus, absent exceptional circumstances such as jury misconduct, the only people who know what happens during deliberations are the jury members themselves. Jurors are instructed, however, to follow the law as given in the instructions, to be fair and impartial, to consult with each other, and to reexamine their views and change their opinion if they are convinced it is erroneous—but not to "surrender your honest convictions to the weight or effect of the evidence solely because of the opinion [576] of your fellow jurors."

Also, if a verdict form with questions is used, as in *Neely v. Fox*, the answers to the questions must be consistent with each other and consistent with the verdict. FED. R. CIV. P. 49(b)(3) [309] & (4) [310].

B. RENDERING A VERDICT IN *NEELY V. FOX*

At 3:25 p.m. on the second day of trial, the jury in *Neely v. Fox* retired to deliberate. The HVAC system at the court was set to automatically shut off at 5:00 p.m., thus it appears that shortly before that time, Judge Guyton checked with the jury to see if they wished to go home or continue to deliberate. The jury informed him that they were almost done with their deliberations and asked to stay until 5:15 [552].

The jury came back at 5:10, and the foreperson stated they had reached a unanimous verdict. Judge Guyton read the verdict form [441] aloud:

We the jury unanimously make the following findings:

Question No. 1: Was the defendant Fox of Oak Ridge, Inc. negligent?

And your answer is: Yes.

Question No. 2: Was the defendant Fox of Oak Ridge's negligence a legal cause of injury to the plaintiff Thomas Neely?

And your answer is: No

And you have gone on and answered No. 3. I will read the [question] of the verdict: What is the total amount of compensatory damages that the plaintiff Thomas Neely is entitled to recover?

And your answer is thirty thousand dollars ($30,000) [568].

The court then excused the jury to wait in the court's conference room, and said to the attorneys: "Would the attorneys like to see the verdict form because the Court has got a problem. ... I just think that maybe the verdict form should have been more detailed. Perhaps the verdict form should have said: If your answer to No. 2 is yes, proceed to No. 3 [559]."

Robert English, counsel for the plaintiff, maintained that the verdict form was inconsistent and thus, "I think I would just move for a judgment notwithstanding the verdict and a new trial." Clint Woodfin, counsel for the defendant, argued that the $30,000 likely represented the medical [560] expenses that were proven in the case and asked for the verdict to stand [569].

The court and counsel discussed how to proceed in perhaps clarifying the jury's intent [570]. In the end, the court confirmed with the jury that their answer to the Question No. 2 was unanimously no, and then asked the foreperson: "given that answer to Question No. 2, why did the jury proceed to answer Question No. 3 [571]?" She replied:

> We felt like it was appropriate for some [compensation] to be given to the plaintiff for what he has gone through so far, because there was negligence on the part of Fox of Oak Ridge [572].

The court then thanked the jury for their service and said the attorneys had not been given permission to contact the jury members to discuss the verdict [572].

The court concluded that the explanation of the foreperson was that "the jury felt that the plaintiff was entitled to be compensated in this case in the amounts of thirty thousand dollars. And so the court is going to enter judgment in that amount."

The court also stated: "I understand there may be motions, written motions. The court will take them up [573]."

On June 22, 2005, judgment [442] was entered for the plaintiff in the amount of $30,000.

QUESTIONS

1. Do you think the answers to the questions on the verdict form were inconsistent? Explain.

2. What do you think led to the inconsistency or confusion in the verdict form?

3. How could the verdict form have been changed to eliminate or at least reduce the possibility of an inconsistent verdict?

4. Since the verdict was in favor of the plaintiff, why do you think plaintiff's counsel argued it was inconsistent and warranted a new trial, while defendant's counsel argued that the verdict should stand?

5. The court decided to enter judgment for $30,000 based on the verdict. Do you think the inconsistency or ambiguity was resolved by the foreperson's explanation as to why the jury went on to answer Question No. 3?

CHAPTER 10

POST-JUDGMENT MOTIONS AND SUBSEQUENT PROCEEDINGS

I.   POST-JUDGMENT MOTIONS

A.   OVERVIEW

After a judgment has been entered, the parties may challenge the judgment in the trial court in several ways.

i. Renewed Motion for Judgment as a Matter of Law—Rule 50

If a party made a motion for judgment as a matter of law before the verdict, the party may renew that motion after a judgment has been entered.   FED. R. CIV. P. 50(b) [326].   Thus, a renewed motion for judgment as a matter of law is based on the same grounds as the original.   The motion must be brought within 28 days of the entry of judgment, or, if the motion addresses an issue not decided by a verdict, within 28 days from when the jury was discharged.   *Id.* The standard for granting a motion for judgment as a matter of law is similar to that of a motion for summary judgment.   *See* FED. R. CIV. P. 56(a) [335].   In determining whether a party is entitled to judgment as a matter of law, the court should (1) disregard any jury determination for which there is no legally sufficient evidentiary basis, (2) consider facts that were established at trial based on legally sufficient evidence, and (3) consider any facts that were established as a matter of law prior to trial based on a motion for summary judgment or adjudication under Rule 56. FED. R. CIV. P. 50(b) advisory committee's note (1993) [325]. The court may then allow judgment to be entered on the verdict, order a new trial, or direct the entry of judgment as a matter of law. FED. R. CIV. P. 50(b) [326]. A motion for judgment as a matter of law may include an alternative or joint motion for new trial. *Id.*

ii. Motion for New Trial—Rule 59

Within 28 days after the entry of judgment, a party may bring a motion for new trial on all or some of the issues that were tried. FED. R. CIV. P. 59(a)(1), (b) [342]. Rule 59 does not list the specific grounds upon which a motion for new trial may be granted. Rather, a new trial may be granted "(A) after a jury trial, for any reason for which a new trial has heretofore been granted in an action at law in federal court; or (B) after a nonjury trial, for any reason for which a rehearing has heretofore been granted in a suit in equity in federal court." FED. R. CIV. P. 59(a)(1)(A) & (B) [343]. Thus, a motion for new trial may be granted on any historically recognized grounds, which include, but are not limited to, claims "that the verdict is against the weight of the evidence, that the damages are excessive, or that, for other reasons, the trial was not fair to the [moving party]." *Montgomery Ward & Co. v. Duncan*, 311 U.S. 243, 251 (1940) [76]. In general, for a trial to be found to be unfair there must be a showing of prejudice or bias—which could be the result of erroneously admitted evidence;

impermissible argument by counsel; outside influence or in intimidation of witnesses or jury members; or judicial or juror misconduct. *See Holmes v. City of Massillon*, 78 F.3d 1041, 1046 (6th Cir. 1996) [121], *cert denied*, 519 U.S. 935 (1996). In addition, a motion for new trial may be based on newly discovered evidence. *See* FED. R. CIV. P. 60(b)(2) [348].

iii. Motion for New Trial Based on an Inconsistent Verdict—Rule 49

If a verdict form with written questions is used at trial, there is the risk of an inconsistent verdict— meaning the answers to the questions are inconsistent with themselves, inconsistent with the verdict, or both. FED. R. CIV. P. 49(b)(2) & (3) [308]. If the answers are consistent with each other, but inconsistent with the verdict, the court may: (1) enter a judgment based on the answers themselves, notwithstanding the verdict; (2) direct the jury to further consider its answers and the verdict; or (3) order a new trial. FED. R. CIV. P. 49(b)(3) [309]. On the other hand, if the answers are inconsistent with each other and one or more is inconsistent with the verdict, the court must either order the jury to reconsider its answers and the verdict or order a new trial. FED. R. CIV. P. 49(b)(4) [310]. When a verdict is rendered that appears to be an inconsistent, it may be difficult for the court to know what immediate action to take. This is because it can be hard to tell right away whether the answers are inconsistent among themselves or just inconsistent with the verdict. Often the answers on the verdict form will simply appear confusing or "wrong" somehow. Hence, if a party believes a judgment has been entered based on an inconsistent verdict, the party should bring a motion for new trial within 28 days of the entry of judgment. FED. R. CIV. P. 59(b) [344]. A new trial is specifically authorized in Rule 49 and may be granted after the court has the time and opportunity to fully consider the matter.

iv. Motion for Relief from Judgment—Rule 60

The court may correct mistakes in the judgment that are clerical or based on an omission or oversight. FED. R. CIV. P. 60(a) [346]. Among the most common Rule 60(a) errors are those involving calculating or transcribing figures, e.g., where the verdict was $500,000, but the judgment states $50,000.

A party may move for relief from judgment under Rule 60(b) [347] based on "(1) mistake, inadvertence, surprise, or excusable neglect; (2) newly discovered evidence that, with reasonable diligence, could not have been discovered in time to move for a new trial under Rule 59(b); (3) fraud . . ., misrepresentation, or misconduct by an opposing party; (4) the judgment is void; (5) the judgment has been satisfied, released, or discharged; (6) it is based on an earlier judgment that has been reversed or vacated; or applying it prospectively is no longer equitable; or (7) any other reason that justifies relief." Motions for relief from judgment are often fact specific and turn on the particular circumstances of the case involved. A fairly common motion under Rule 60(b) is a motion to vacate a default judgment on the ground that service was improper, and thus the court did not have jurisdiction over the defendant—rendering the judgment void. *Mann v. Castiel*, 681 F.3d 368, 372 (D.C. Cir. 2012) [117]; *see* Chapter 3, section II(f), p. 38.

B.   MOTION FOR NEW TRIAL IN *NEELY V. FOX*

On June 30, 2006, the plaintiff moved for a new trial [443] pursuant to Federal Rules of Civil Procedure 49(b) and 59. In his memorandum in support [452], the plaintiff attached the verdict form in which the jury answered "No" to Question 2— "Was the defendant Fox of Oak Ridge's negligence a legal cause of injury to the plaintiff Thomas Neely?"—but then, in Question 3 [447], the jury awarded Neely $30,000. The plaintiff maintained the verdict was "inconsistent with the answers under Rule 49(b) and it reflects a lack of understanding and state of general confusion on the part of the jury [444] [under Rule 59]."

The plaintiff pointed out that, under Tennessee law, a defendant is not liable for negligence unless all elements of the tort have been proven, including the element of legal cause. Thus, the plaintiff argued that the verdict of $30,000 was inconsistent with the jury's answer that the defendant's negligence was not the legal cause of his injuries, and thus a new trial was required under Rule 49(b).

The plaintiff also argued that a new trial was warranted under Rule 59 because the verdict form reflected a lack of understanding or general confusion on the part of the jury. This lack of understanding and confusion was demonstrated by the fact that the "[j]ury found simultaneously for and against the Defendant in finding the defendant was not the legal cause of Plaintiff's damages, yet still liable to the Plaintiff for damages sought [451]."

The defendant opposed the motion for new trial, arguing (1) the verdict was not inconsistent; (2) even if it were inconsistent, the court was required to uphold the verdict if possible; and (3) any alleged inconsistency was harmless [456]. The defendant maintained that "clearly, the jury unanimously believed that the plaintiff's credibility had been impeached to the point that any expert proof supporting injuries was given little or no weight" and that the relatively small award of $30,000 reflected that belief [454]. The defendant also argued that by entering judgment on the $30,000 verdict the court gave effect to the intention of the jury, which it was required by law to do [457]. Lastly, the defendant argued that under Federal Rule of Civil Procedure 61, any error by the court in entering judgment on the verdict was harmless because it did not affect the plaintiff's substantial rights. The defendant contended that, on the contrary, "The jury's verdict and the entry of the judgment affected the substantial rights of the **defendant** who could make the argument that if it was not the legal cause of damages to the plaintiff, then no judgment should be entered against it [455]" (emphasis in original).

After conducting a hearing [460] on the motion for new trial, the court issued a memorandum and order granting the plaintiff's motion for new trial and vacating the judgment [464]. The court stated that when it read the verdict form it determined the answers to Questions 2 and 3 appeared to be inconsistent. The court had attempted to resolve the apparent inconsistency by questioning the jury foreperson, who explained that even though they answered "No" to the question of whether the defendant's negligence was the legal cause of the plaintiff's injuries, they went on to award him $30,000 because "[w]e felt like it was appropriate for some [compensation] to be given to the plaintiff for what he has gone through so far, because there was negligence on the part of Fox in Oak Ridge [461]." Based on this explanation, the court "determined that what the jury intended to say was that the defendant was the legal cause of $30,000 of the plaintiff's claimed damages, but not the legal cause of the other claimed damages." Further, "wanting to give effect to what the court perceived to be the intent of the jury, then entered a verdict for the plaintiff in the amount of $30,000 [462]."

In the memorandum and order, the court determined that despite its conclusion at the time of trial, the verdict was inconsistent and reflected the fact that the jury did not follow the law as instructed and was confused when it completed the verdict form [465]. The court reasoned: "The explanation given by the foreperson for the inconsistent verdict can only be accepted as resolving the inconsistency with the use of the Court's subjective interpretation of the meaning of the foreperson's comment. However, the verdict of the jury must not be such that the subjective interpretation of the Court is required to discern it [465]." The court also rejected the defendant's argument that a new trial should not be granted because any error was harmless under Rule 61 [350], finding "that the overriding issue is the integrity of the process itself [463]."

QUESTIONS

1. If a party did not move for a judgment as a matter of law prior to the verdict, may the party move for a judgment as a matter of law after judgment has been entered? Explain.

2. In a motion for new trial under Rule 59, what generally must be found for a trial to be considered unfair?

3. What are the court's options under Rule 49 [305] if the answers on the verdict form are consistent with each other, but inconsistent with the verdict?

4. Is a motion by a party required to correct a clerical error under Rule 60(a) [346]?

5. In its memorandum and order granting the motion for new trial and vacating the judgment [464], the court noted that the verdict form was deficient in at least one respect. In what respect was it deficient?

6.   According to the court, how was the verdict form also potentially deficient?

II. SUBSEQUENT PROCEEDINGS

A.   OVERVIEW

Whether or not post-trial motions are filed, the entry of a judgment does not automatically end the civil action.

1.   Appeal of the Judgment

First, if the judgment is final—if it "ends the litigation on the merits and leaves nothing for the court to do but execute the judgment." *Caitlin v. United States*, 324 U.S. 229, 233 (1945) [78]. The losing or "aggrieved" party may appeal the judgment. *See* 28 U.S.C. § 1291 [13]. An appeal is not an opportunity to retry the case, however. The appellate court does not hear additional testimony or receive additional evidence. It reviews the record of proceedings in the trial court. The party filing an appeal, usually called the "appellant," must convince the appellate court that (1) there was error below, and (2) that error requires reversal of the judgment. The first step involves evaluating the decision below based on the applicable standard of review. Standards of review define the amount of deference the decision will be accorded. For example, findings of fact are given substantial deference by appellate courts and will be upheld unless they are shown, for example, to be "clearly erroneous." On the other hand, conclusions of law made by the trial court are not accorded deference and will be reviewed "de novo"—meaning anew. After all, if it is a question of law and not of fact, appellate judges are in as good a position to decide the matter. Determining whether there was error below is only the first step in the process. If the appellate court finds error, it must next determine if the error requires that the judgment be reversed or if the error is "harmless." This involves evaluating whether and how the error affected the result in the case. For example, if the appellate court determines that the jury clearly would have reached the same verdict even if certain evidence had not been erroneously admitted, the error will usually be considered harmless.

2. Enforcement of the Judgment—Rule 69

The fact that a judgment was entered and not appealed does not automatically mean the judgment will be paid. There is no automatic teller machine in which to deposit and cash a money judgment. In other words, judicial remedies are not self-enforcing. In some cases, parties with judgments against them voluntarily pay the judgments in full. If not, the party holding the judgment, known as the "judgment creditor," will need to enforce the judgment by obtaining a "writ of execution" from the clerk of court. FED. R. CIV. P. 69(a)(1) [351]; see, e.g., E.D. TENN. L.R. 69.1 [159]. After the writ is issued, the procedure on execution must comport with state law. FED. R. CIV. P. 69(a)(1). In Tennessee, where *Neely v. Fox* was filed, as in most states, a writ of execution "is simply an order directing [an officer] to levy upon and sell the judgment debtor's property identified in the writ that is not statutorily exempt" and is now "the customary vehicle for enforcing money judgments." *Keep Fresh Filters, Inc. v. Reguli*, 888 S.W.2d 437, 443 [125] (Tenn. Ct. App. 1994). The levy of execution, in turn, "is the officer's act of appropriating or singling out the debtor's property for the satisfaction of a debt." *Ingle v. Head*, No. W2006–02690–COA-R3–CV, 2007 WL 4530825 at *8 n. 9 (Tenn. Ct. App. Dec. 26, 2007) [9].

If the proceeds from the writ of execution are insufficient to satisfy the judgment, the judgment creditor may need to continue going after the property of the defendant until sufficient funds have been collected. Thus it is very important to know what assets the defendant has and to attempt to levy on sufficient assets as quickly as possible. This is also why post-judgment discovery may be important to uncover assets. *See* FED. R. CIV. P. 69(a)(2) [352]. Once new or additional assets are identified, the judgment creditor can obtain another writ and start the execution process over again. It is also possible to garnish an individual's wages by obtaining and serving a writ of garnishment upon their employer, who will then deduct and pay over to the judgment creditor a portion of each paycheck of the defendant.

3. Retrial

If the court grants a motion for new trial, the civil action is reset on the court's calendar—meaning a new trial date is assigned and the parties and counsel must begin preparing for a second trial. An order granting a new trial is "interlocutory in nature" and thus is not immediately appealable. *Allied Chemical Corp. v. Daiflon, Inc.*, 449 U.S. 33, 34 (1980) [93]. Indeed, unlike a final appealable order that "ends the litigation on the merits and leaves nothing for the court to do but execute the judgment" *Caitlin v. United States*, 324 U.S. 229, 233 (1945) [78], an order granting a new trial essentially begins the case anew. With the advantage of hindsight, counsel may produce additional evidence or witnesses; they may also conduct additional discovery—as long as it is not repetitive, cumulative, or unduly burdensome, FED. R. CIV. P. 26(b)(2)(C) [233], file new dispositive motions, employ different trial strategies, and enter into settlement negotiations.

B.   SUBSEQUENT PROCEEDINGS IN *NEELY V. FOX*

On July 24, 2006, the court granted the plaintiff's motion for a new trial and vacated the judgment [464]. Just over a month later, on August 31, the court set a new trial date for February 6, 2007 [157]. The parties' pretrial preparations appear to have progressed smoothly with no disputes that needed court involvement. On November 11, 2006, the plaintiff filed his final witness list, which included two additional witnesses that had not been listed for the previous trial—the plaintiff's wife, Sandra Neely, and Julian Nadolsky, Ed.D., a vocational expert, *see Black v. Roadway Express, Inc.*, 297 F.3d 445, 454 (6th Cir. 2002) [73]. The final pretrial conference [157] was set for January 31, 2007, and then reset for January 30, 2007. It appears, however, that the court did not hold the final pretrial conference. Rather, the parties notified the court they had reached a settlement [157], and on February 15, counsel for both parties filed a formal notice of settlement [468]. The settlement was not filed with the court and remains confidential. Once parties decide to settle a civil action with a simple lump sum payment, the contract of settlement can be drawn up, signed by the parties, and payment exchanged for a release of claims. On May 15, 2007, the parties filed a Stipulation of Dismissal with Prejudice of Thomas Neely's civil action [469] against Fox of Oak Ridge and Benjamin Curd.[21] On that day, the case was closed.

QUESTIONS

1. If the losing party in a jury trial believes that its evidence was stronger than the other side's, would you recommend that the party appeal the judgment? Explain.

2. What should counsel for a judgment creditor do if they are not sure that the judgment will be paid in full?

3. Why do you think the plaintiff planned to call the additional witnesses, Sandra Neely and Julian Nadolsky, Ed.D?

---

[21] Remember that prior to the first trial, Benjamin Curd had been dismissed [459] without prejudice—meaning he could be added again as a defendant. *See* Chapter 8, section V.

4. Why do you think *Neely v. Fox* settled before going to trial a second time?

5. What was the effect of dismissing Fox of Oak Ridge and Benjamin Curd "with prejudice?"